Praise for Blended but not Broken

With the obvious crumbling of the foundation of the American home so easily visible today, thousands of blended families are begging for help. The secular world is luring a whole generation into moral and spiritual bankruptcy. But, thank God, the Word of the Lord, the Holy Scripture, is enjoying a new popularity. It is with great pleasure that I recommend to you the book **_Blended But Not Broken_**. Pam Rohr is someone who has proven the principles in this book, and has earned the right to speak on this subject. This is a book that will literally transform blended families. With so much working against the family in our society, it is wonderful to see this shining light that will show you the way in which to go – God's way. The book is presented with candor and insight that will truly touch your heart. As the Holy Spirit guides you through these chapters your family will truly be transformed. This is one of those books you will be unable to put down until you have completed reading it. May the Lord bless you as you take a journey of faith through these pages. Your life will never be the same.

Pastor Rick Bloom
Pacific Christian Center
Santa Maria, CA

BLENDED *but not* BROKEN

*Hope and Encouragement
for Blended Families*

Pamela Rohr

Dedication

This book is dedicated with love and highest respect to my husband and best friend, Ron. I honor you for raising my son (now our son) and for taking in my brother's son when he needed a home, love, and guidance after the passing of his father. While we knew it wouldn't be easy, you jumped in wholeheartedly.

Though we certainly made our share of mistakes and had many ups and downs, God has been very faithful to us and the fruit of our efforts has been rewarded. We have four wonderful children, all gifts from the Lord any parent would be proud to claim as their own. I thank you for your integral example, and for doing the right thing, even when it was not the popular thing, and for being an involved husband and father.

You are truly my gift from the Lord. You saw things in me I never saw in myself, and you encouraged me to do things I never thought I could do. Thank you.

Contents

Psalm 128: 1,2

"Blessed are all who fear the Lord, who walk in his ways.
You will eat the fruit of your labor; blessings and prosperity will be yours."

Introduction

One of the key objectives of this book is to bring you **hope**.

Do you sometimes feel you are the only family struggling in your effort at making your blended family blend... and you wonder why? Appearances can be deceiving, you are not alone.

In this book you will read the stories of other blended families who have experienced the same problems and pitfalls you are now experiencing. You will be encouraged in your own family as you learn of other survival stories. Making your blended family work is worth the effort and time it takes.

You will be rewarded for your diligence if you do not give up. I know many times we are tempted to quit because our situation seems to drag on forever, but if you will follow these tried and proven principles set forth in this book, you will find successful results.

Chapter 1

Step vs. Blended

"I will be a Father to you, and you will be my sons and daughters, says the Lord Almighty." 2 Corinthians 6:18

My husband and daughter love to make smoothies. They get all of the ingredients together: strawberries, pineapple, bananas, yogurt—whatever they can find. They start on the first button of the blender and work their way up to "blend." When they feel the ingredients are sufficiently mixed, they pour just a little into a glass to try it. They discuss whether it needs anything else and what that might be.

They mix the ingredients long enough for each to keep its own flavor while enhancing the flavors of the other ingredients. They have mastered when to go from one button to the next by the sound of the ingredients being mixed. They blend it just right so that it will be smooth but will have an occasional chunk of strawberry, for example, which is covered with the flavors of the other fruit. Yum!

Blenders are used to bring otherwise separate ingredients together to make a new creation in a combination of the separate parts. That is what blended families try to do. Two separate families not bound together by blood combine to form a new family in which everyone gets along. How can they blend? A family cannot put itself into a blender to produce a desired result. They must go through a **process.**

This process is determined by many factors and will be as unique as the members of your family. The length of time the process takes depends on the commitment level of each individual. Do the members want to blend and become a family? Just because the parents wanted the marriage, don't assume the children are happy about it. Are they resistant to or even sabotaging good relationships from developing?

What outside influences are affecting your new family? Are there people who would like nothing better than to see your family disintegrate before it has a chance to blend? What are they doing to put additional pressure or stress on your family? And, do you pray together as a family? As you can see, there are many factors that can either help or hinder the blending process.

What makes a blended family so different from a first-time, "no step-relationships" involved family? The adults are the same. They married because they are in love. But the children and their needs are added considerations to be made.

The stepparent and child relationships, as well as the stepsibling relationships, are what make the blended family so difficult. We don't automatically love our spouse's child—after all, we didn't bring that child into the world. Furthermore, siblings don't necessarily take to each other simply because they live in the same house. Living in the same house might be the only thing they have in common; they don't have a history together or share both parents as a unifying factor.

Some say that blending a stepfamily is not possible; that all one can hope for is amicable relationships without a true feeling of connectedness. I strongly disagree! I have witnessed stepdaughters wanting their stepmoms with them in the delivery room to experience the birth of their first baby and sons asking their stepdads to be the Best Man at their wedding.

Becoming a well-blended family is a process and takes differing amounts of time, depending upon the members. But it is certainly attainable.

I prefer to call our stepfamily a blended family. "Step" sounds cold and indifferent to me. It sounds like some members are held at arm's length. Blended, however, gets the point across that you were not always a family but you are one now and want to be identified with one another.

Blended Family

The process of blending a family can be compared to the buttons on a blender which are grate, chop, grind, stir, puree, mix, and finally, blend. Blending a family takes time. Don't expect too much too soon. Allow the children to set their own pace with their new stepparent. Too much affection or too much discipline too soon can actually push them away from you.

The first button, "grate," means to irritate. After the honeymoon period, there will come a time of grating on each other's nerves as you begin to notice things you didn't know before the marriage. Your stepchild doesn't say hello to you, in fact, pretends you are not even there when you walk into the room. This can be irritating.

Next is "chop." Family members might begin to experience a feeling of being cut down by blows, cut into small bits, cut off, or displaced. They may feel they have lost the importance they once held in their first family. A child who was the firstborn in his family before it merged might find himself a middle child now. He may feel he has lost firstborn status and the privileges and responsibilities that come with it. He feels he has been "chopped down" to a lower level than he previously held.

The next is "grind." This button makes you feel like ground beef, crushed into bits or pulverized. You begin to wonder, "What have I done and is there any way out of this family?" The happy family you dreamed about is becoming "them against you." You might feel your spouse sides with his children against you or that you are a referee between your spouse and your child. It seems no matter what you do, someone is mad at you.

The fourth button is "stir," which means to agitate. In a blender, the separate ingredients are agitating one another like iron sharpening iron to produce the desired result. Even in first families there is some conflict. It is multiplied exponentially in blended families due to the unique variables inherent in them. You don't approve of how your stepchild disregards the rule that everyone else abides by, which may be to clean up his own dishes. You've become a thorn in his side as you enforce the rule. But, he is also sharpening you in that you are learning patience and perseverance. You are stirring each other up.

The fifth is puree. Ever felt like you've been strained and stressed to the point of not wanting to go on? The day-to-day pressure has mounted and you feel like "mush." These types of days happen to all of us. Trying to keep peace with a teen with an attitude from "you-know-where" can be exhausting. When you feel pureed, take care of yourself.

Do something for you. Talk to a trusted friend, pray, have some time alone with your spouse, go for a walk, write a letter describing what you are going through (it has been shown that writing your thoughts down can relieve quite a bit of stress), or call a family meeting.

Next is "mix," which means to join or combine. This is a place of connecting with the other members and having a feeling of belonging. It's making two families into one and experiencing a true attachment with one another. You wouldn't dream of missing your stepchild's baseball game simply because you love him and want to support him.

Finally, the "blend" button. This is mixing and mingling so as to produce the desired result of unity, combining and merging. The goal in a blended family must be to "blend." You might not attain it to the level you would like. But, if your goal is not blending, you never will. You will fall short of reaching a sense of having a family that belongs to one another.

La Dolce Vita is a fine coffee made from four different blends. Our son, Keenan, is a Roaster of some of the finest coffees and receives his beans from all over the world. After receiving a particular coffee, say, Ethiopian, he roasts it in the roasting drum for the exact specified time to bring out its own unique flavor. To make La Dolce Vita, he combines four different blends to make one coffee. He will mix them, mingle them, join them, and merge them into one new blend. They are good by themselves but they are also good together.

That is the goal of a blended family. To join, unify and mix the individual people so they will be good together. It takes time in a family because people are involved and they have their own personalities, desires, emotions, hurts and dreams. The blending process must be at a comfortable pace with each individual member. You might blend more quickly with one stepchild than with another.

Don't think your blending process is going to happen quickly. If it does, you are fortunate. But pushing your family members to blend before they are ready for it is like taking the lid off of a pressure cooker while it is cooking—it will blow up in your face!

Our blending took about 15 years because we had very little help and guidance. If we knew then what we know now, the process would have been shortened. That is why this book is written; to help you reach "blending" with a lot fewer headaches and heartaches than we had. But it was worth the work and the staying power it took to get there. So relax, be patient, and trust that your family will get there too.

5

Grafted In

Being a member of a blended family is similar to belonging to the family of God. Just as a divorce or the death of a spouse can leave us wounded, so can trying to survive in a world where there is no feeling of community. Families no longer live close by and neighbors keep to themselves. We truly feel we are on our own. But belonging to the family of God and/or being accepted into a new family can change all that. The following is a beautiful story of a man becoming a dad by accepting as his own a daughter not born to him.

After Jill's divorce, she felt dumped, used and abused. She was determined never to trust another man with her love and her heart again…and then she met Sam. Their relationship began as friends but as time went on they found they wanted to enjoy each other's company more and more. Jill's only daughter, Lisa, liked Sam all right but wasn't sure she wanted him as anything more than just her mom's friend. Her heart had been broken the day her dad left. He had said he would call and come to see her often. He only came once in the years following the divorce and rarely ever called.

The news that mom and Sam were engaged was earthshaking information to Lisa. She experienced a range of emotions from fear of being demoted in the eyes of her mom; to an inner hope that maybe they could become a real family. She questioned whether she could ever really love Sam and would she ever like living with him? She was used to it being just her and mom.

In the months leading up to the wedding, Sam began to take a real interest in Lisa. Sam and Jill began to include Lisa in their outings and would try to do things they knew Lisa would enjoy. Sometimes, when Jill was busy, and Lisa wanted, Sam would take her out for an ice cream or a romp at the park. Lisa was beginning to like having Sam around but she still wasn't sure she wanted him to live with them.

The wedding day came and went. It was different having Sam around all the time, but Lisa was starting to like it. She felt more secure and not so concerned with adult issues such as "It's my job to take care of mom." She was beginning to relax and enjoy being a kid.

After some time, Lisa began to wonder if she could call Sam "Dad." She approached him with the question one afternoon and of course, he was elated. Her parents then told her that they had discussed the possibility of Sam adopting Lisa to become his own daughter. She kind of liked the idea. They could become a real family.

The legal proceedings began and the day came for them to go before the judge who would either grant or deny the adoption. They had paid a great price in attorney's fees and had even paid a sum of money to her biological dad so he would be willing to let her become another man's daughter.

Court day had arrived. The judge cleared the courtroom of all strangers. The only people present were family and close friends who cared about the outcome.

As they stood before the judge, he first asked Sam why he wanted to adopt Lisa. He shared from his heart his love for her and Jill. He wanted to become a father to her with the same responsibilities and rights other fathers have. He wanted most of all, to convince Lisa of his love and that he would never hurt her intentionally. He wanted her to feel safe and secure with him.

When the judge asked Lisa if she would accept him as her father she replied that she already had. She said he was the only man in her life who wanted to be her dad and he did all the things that dads do. She asked the judge to please let him become her daddy.

By the time the judge spoke to Jill, she was crying tears of joy over the love expressed by the two most important people in her life. The judge didn't have to spend much time with her because her joy spoke loud and clear.

When the gavel came down announcing the adoption was granted, shouts of overwhelming delight were heard in the usually quiet halls of the court. They had a wonderful celebration! But, the icing on the cake was when Sam presented his "little girl" with a gift he had chosen especially for her. It was a beautiful necklace with two gold hearts hanging from it to signify how their hearts had become forever joined. She has cherished it ever since, but the best gift she received that day was a father who loved her and would continue to be involved in her life.

This is a picture of Father God inviting us to become a part of His family. He paid a huge price for us through the death of His Son, Jesus Christ. By His wounds (the beating He took), we are healed, and by the shedding of His blood, our sins are forgiven. None of us can ever be good enough to get ourselves to heaven. If we could do this, then Jesus died in vain. It is His blood spiritually applied to our lives that allows us to become the children of God. He readily accepts us just like Sam accepted Lisa to be his child.

Once we belong to the family of God, we are connected to God's other children and they are now our brothers and sisters. We belong to a community of believers who are there for us. We should take care of each other. This is how a blended family should work. All members are important simply because they belong to the family. What you would do for your own child should be what you would do for your spouse's child because that child belongs to the family.

If you have not been grafted into the family of God and would like to, you can stop right here and say this simple prayer:

> Heavenly Father, I admit I am a sinner and am in need of a Savior (Romans 3:23). I believe in my heart that Jesus died on the cross for my sins (1Corinthians 15:3,4) and I confess that Jesus is Lord. I believe in my heart that God raised Him from the dead so that I can be saved (Romans 10:9).

If you just took this step of faith and joined the family of God, congratulations! You will need to get into a good Bible-believing church so you can grow spiritually and connect with some brothers and sisters who can be there for you and you for them.

As in a blended family or the family of God, we are not blood related but we are still a family. Spiritual ties can sometimes become stronger than blood ties. Our attitude must be one of love and acceptance of others whether they are blood related or not. If you do as the Word tells us, "be kind and compassionate to one another, forgiving each other, just as in Christ God forgave you" (Ephesians 4:32) you will see some major changes take place.

You must give respect in order to receive it. It cannot be demanded; it is earned. Realize it is not about your comfort but about making your family work. It was not comfortable for Jesus to die on the cross for us to become His brothers and sisters but He did it anyway. Sacrifice for your family and you will be greatly rewarded.

The key then to helping your family blend is "Don't give up!" Take on an attitude of caring for your stepchildren and be an example of love to them. As you attempt to do the right thing by them, they will realize it. They may never come to call you Mom or Dad but you can reach the goal of a mutually satisfying relationship.

Spotlight On The Blending Process

Instant Replay: Blending is a process that takes differing lengths of time depending on the family members and circumstances. It is possible to mix, blend, and enjoy a sense of belonging within your blended family.

Self Examination: Referring to the buttons on the blender, where do I feel I am? What can I personally do to help our family blend? Am I showing respect and expecting respect in every relationship?

Action: I will share this chapter with my family and use it as a tool for discussion. Some questions we will discuss are: Where do you feel we are when referring to the buttons on the blender? Do you feel respected as an important part of the family? Why or why not? What can we do as a family to help us get to the blended button quicker? What can we do differently to foster a sense of belonging with one other?

Chapter 2

The Promise of "I Do"

"And they will become one flesh." Genesis 2:24

The telephone's screech pierced the silence of the sleepy night. It woke up my husband Ron and me for the third time that unending evening. We finally fell back to sleep and hoped not to hear from my ex-husband again. It was now 3:00 A.M. and we both had to get up for work in just a few hours. We were exhausted. This had become a common occurrence causing us to feel harassed and intruded upon in our own home. This was before cell phones and monitoring calls was difficult.

Seemingly from the day Ron and I spoke our wedding vows, our exes had teamed up to destroy our newly formed family. They not only tried to divide us but they tried to turn our children against us. They told our children things about us to get them on "their side" and to dissuade them from liking their new stepparent. No price seemed too high in their determination to divide and separate us.

We had to make a choice. Would we continue living in the same area as our ex-spouses and their families, or would we move away so that our new family could have a chance?

Since second marriages have an even higher rate of divorce than first marriages, we had to decide from the start that nothing was going to come between us. We really didn't expect our exes to respond to our marriage the way they did, particularly since we were both divorced before we met each other. We knew that if we didn't stick together we would be at war with each other due to the stress and tension that was being created from outside forces.

So we made the tough decision to move away from our family and friends. We were expecting our only child together at that time, so the emotion of having to leave my mom and brother, our aunts, uncles and cousins to move to another state was overwhelming. But we knew we couldn't continue under the stress these outside pressures were having on our family.

We determined that protecting our marriage covenant was more important to us than living in the area where we had made our home. It was very hard leaving our life, family, church and friends, but it had become a matter of marital survival! We had to leave the past behind and separate ourselves from it all in order to gain a new beginning and a happy future together.

The key to any successful marriage is **commitment.** Therefore, we clung to each other. We devoted ourselves to each other, our children, and to the vows we had made before God the day we said, "I do."

A Promise Is a Continual Choice

Marriage is a covenant between a man and a woman that is designed to last "until death do us part." It is an agreement or contract made by two individuals to do certain things and keep certain promises. In a marriage covenant, both parties express their personal commitment to the relationship by making promises. Each person is expected to keep his or her part of the agreement. God honors the covenant and His desire is for us to keep our promises to each another. When we do this, He is free to bless our union.

Some people enter marriage with the view that if it doesn't work out, they could "just get a divorce." They don't understand that love is a choice, a decision to stay committed; an act of your will, it is not just a feeling. All marriages have ups and downs. But, when the couple is not fully committed to making their marriage work, it usually doesn't. They have an escape plan in the back of their mind from the start.

Marriage is a covenant where you freely decide to commit. You must make up your mind to commit to it in good times and bad. Your marriage doesn't just affect you. I found out through my divorce that there were many lives devastated because our marriage didn't last.

Your marriage commitment cannot be based on feelings alone. Good feelings will come and go. Sometimes you will feel in love with your mate and sometimes you won't. It wasn't until after Ron's divorce and he dedicated himself to the Lord, that he had a revelation about commitment through the song by Don Francisco that says "Love is not a feeling but an **act of your will**."

In Covenant, the "Mine" and "Yours" <u>Should</u> Become "Ours"...

When a couple marries, promises are exchanged to love, honor, and cherish each another. Certain terms are agreed upon to include future events that could occur. Vows are made until death do us part, for better or for worse, in sickness and in health.

The two partners in marriage now bring their individual belongings together to become joint property. Salaries are combined; bank accounts, cars, furniture and homes are shared equally. Many times in a second marriage children are a part of the deal—my child now becomes a part of your life and vice versa. Alimony and child support are included in the family budget.

In Biblical times, when a covenant was made between two tribes they would exchange bodily fluids (usually blood) as a sign that they had a treaty with each other. If another tribe attacked their covenant tribe,, they would pool all of their resources and fight side by side to ensure victory. They would **literally lay down their lives** for their covenant tribe. Whatever they owned was the property of the other tribe, should they need it or ask for it.

That is a great picture of a marriage relationship. In marriage, you exchange bodily fluids to consummate your covenant and what was once mine now becomes ours. Everything is to be shared mutually and each partner is to care for their spouse as they would their own self. Nothing is to be withheld from one another. When something is withheld, you can bet problems will occur. Why? Because you are in **covenant** with each other. You should be so committed that you are willing to lay down your life for your spouse.

In today's terms, that means not just thinking of your own needs, but those of your spouse. This is the only family relationship that you **chose** and it requires a covenant with commitment.

Protect Your Covenant Relationship

Ecclesiastes 4:9-12 describes a great working friendship. Your partner should be your very best friend. Who else have you made covenant with until "death do you part"? Even your children will leave you one day and cleave to their own spouse. The above-mentioned verse says: "Two are better than one, because they have a good return for their work: If one falls down his friend can help him up. But pity the man who falls and has no one to help him up! Also, if two lie down together, they will keep warm. But how can one keep warm alone? Though one may be overpowered, two can defend themselves. A cord of three strands is not quickly broken." The three parts to the strand are you, your spouse and the Holy Spirit. Don't allow anything or anyone to come between you, your partner, and the Holy Spirit.

In the garden, God declared, "It is not good that man should be alone" and so he gave Eve to Adam. He intends for the marriage covenant to be honored above every other relationship. This is crucial to realize in a blended family.

In a blended family, it's very easy to keep your relationship with your child as first and most important. After all, you've been together longer, you've been through a lot together and your child may have satisfied emotional needs for you that should have been fulfilled by your first spouse.

You may be so emotionally tied to your child, like I was, that it could be interfering with the bonding of you and your spouse. It can become you and your child against the world (and most unfortunately, your new marriage partner). The child certainly doesn't want to take second place to your spouse and often-times will do everything he or she can to maintain the relationship with you "just the way it's always been."

My little boy, Keenan, and I were so close that it was very hard for him to release me to be anything but his mom. This caused guilt in me so I wanted to prove to him that he would always be very important to me. Consequently, I overcompensated in some areas.

He once told me, after he was grown, that if he had known at the time of our marriage that he would have to become second to my husband, he would have done what he could to stop the marriage from taking place. He was only 6 years old when we married and he wanted to remain number one in my life.

Your child probably has the same feelings. It's very important to let the children know they are still a very high priority to you. Over a period of time you can teach and demonstrate to them why the marriage covenant relationship you have entered is God's design and therefore of utmost importance to building the family. You need to show your child how it benefits him to honor your marriage covenant as God designed it. This will train him to be committed in his own marriage.

It's very important for you to understand that this is part of the ***relationship growing process.*** You cannot expect it to happen overnight and it may take several years, depending on your family dynamics. You must choose the right time to express the importance of your covenant relationship to your child. Please refer to the Bonding Process in Chapter 3 and the discipline/relationship progression in Chapter 7.

When the marriage comes first, everyone profits. As you cleave to your spouse and become united, your child will benefit tremendously. He will become more secure in realizing this family is going to stay together. He will relax and be able to take on the role of the child and be free to become who he is. As he sees his parent make a commitment to the family, it will be easier for him to make one as well.

Children Benefit from the Protected Covenant

As we said, when you marry, all of your spouse's possessions and debts become yours as well. Responsibility for the children becomes shared. You take on a responsibility for them that you did not have before.

Mary, Joseph, and Jesus are a perfect example. Joseph was Jesus' stepfather but Joseph accepted Jesus as his own; he provided for him, protected him, taught him, loved him, and disciplined him. Jesus was Mary's natural child but God had chosen Joseph to be His stepfather with all the rights and responsibilities of a biological father.

If you believe God has put you and your spouse together, then your union is for the good of your children, as well as you. It took me years to believe this. I didn't think my husband loved my son, based on the way he disciplined. So, I took on the attitude that my son was mine and I could handle all that concerns him. I didn't need or want my new husband's "interference." (However, if your spouse is abusing your child, get help). Because my husband and child sensed this "he's my child" attitude in me, it added to the strife and division in our home.

It is never wise to say, either verbally or through body language, that your child is not also your partner's. It just breeds division. In my case, both my husband and son could sense that I was not totally releasing my son to become my husband's child as well. Your child must see that you and your spouse are working together or they will use any inroad to come between you.

Trust and Covenant

When you got married, you most likely trusted your spouse. But what makes the second family different from the first are the step children involved. After you have lived with your partner for a while and have observed them relate to you, and especially your children, distrust can become a major issue, especially if communication is not open and honest.

Since I didn't think Ron really loved Keenan and he felt like I wasn't backing him up when he did discipline Keenan, distrust set in on both sides of our relationship. We all lost out, but the one who suffered most was my son because he was caught in the middle. This was a *marriage* issue, not a *parenting* issue. We should have addressed the core problems, which were my believing Ron didn't love Keenan, and our mutual distrust.

We should have worked on our marriage and gotten down to the main problem, which was lack of trust toward each other. We would have had a lot less friction between us over my son had we dealt with the core issue and worked on that.

Since communication had become so difficult for us, particularly in this area where Keenan was concerned, it seemed easier to just not bring it up. That was a mistake, because in the long run, things bothered us that shouldn't have, and we ended up with more problems than necessary. Had we dealt with the true issues, we could have spared ourselves much grief.

Trust and commitment are the **foundation** of your covenant. Your marriage will be rocky if you do not fully trust each other and are not totally committed to each other.

Restoring Trust

If you believe distrust is a problem in your marriage, seek help. If the two of you can't talk about the issues with each other, like we couldn't, get a third party involved. Get a trusted friend or pastor to help you work through this area so that you can trust once again.

Get to the core issue, don't skirt around it by accusing each other of things that bother you. Instead, work as a couple who is interested in getting to the root of the problem and move in the direction of getting it solved. If your problems are serious, you might consider a professional counselor. Your marriage is worth the effort and expense!

Recommit yourselves to your marriage relationship, ask for forgiveness, and freely give it. Open communication, done with respect, will help you to understand the other's issues, and where both of you are "coming from." Unless you start talking and getting to the root issues, your problems will not go away, they will only grow.

Oftentimes what seems to be a parenting problem is really a marital problem. Until you and your covenant partner can work together, you will be dealing with issues that come up that are really just a symptom of the larger problem: your lack of communication, trust, and unity.

Marriage is meant for the two to become one in every area. Your parenting job should become easier because you have a helpmate and someone to "bounce things off." But more times than not, in second marriages, parenting becomes even harder simply because the couple does not unite through communication to work out their differences until complete agreement is reached.

If you do not trust your partner, you have a choice. Continue the way you are or work on the relationship until you do. Get to the root: Why don't you trust him? What steps can be done to regain trust and get you both working together rather than each of you doing your own thing?

For a successful marriage covenant, you must be committed. Then, work on maintaining trust and unity through communication so that your union will be strong, healthy and enjoyable. Marriage was meant to be the most fulfilling relationship you have.

Spotlight On My Marriage

Instant Replay: Marriage is the only family relationship you have that is a covenant. Therefore, it must be first. Be committed to developing trust and unity so that your union will be all that you hoped it would be.

Self Examination: How am I committed to my marriage and what am I doing to ensure its success?

Action: What can I do this week to show my spouse that they are "Number One" to me? Some suggestions: Plan a special evening out for just the two of you. Perhaps you could send the children to the neighbors so the two of you could have an uninterrupted night at home, alone, for some talking and romance. Talk about the early days of your relationship, how you met, what attracted you to each other. Reminisce about some funny things that have happened to you as a couple and share a laugh together.

Chapter 3

Letting Go of the Past

"...and by His wounds we are healed." Isaiah 53:5

Marriage is becoming one in flesh and in self. Self in Webster's dictionary refers to the identity, character or essential qualities of a person. So...the two shall become one (united) not only physically but also in their identities. They shall be known as a couple.

When a man and woman become one flesh physically and emotionally, they are bonded to each other. When this bond is severed through divorce (which means in Hebrew "a cutting away so that the one becomes two again") the results can be very painful. It has been said that divorce is more painful to endure than a death, but in reality, it is a death. It's the death of a marriage and a family.

Due to the fact that you are remarried and in a blended family, you have been injured along life's way. If you endured the pain of a divorce, or have been widowed, you may have some hurts that need mending. None of us can journey through a lifetime without receiving wounds and hurts along the way.

Wound Anyone?

Since we all have been wounded, what we do with those wounds is the ultimate question. Will we nurse them, deny them, and pretend they don't affect us, or will we deal with them and move on? The key to our healing is forgiveness.

You may have wounds from your childhood, your previous marriage or your current one. Many of us have been rejected, abandoned, slandered, ridiculed and abused. If you are harboring unforgiveness, it will eventually be the thing that holds you captive. Don't let it.

You might think that you have dealt with all your past hurts, but if you think about the person or situation and get a knot in your stomach, or you want to defame their character, or you want to see them "get theirs", then you have not completely forgiven and been healed.

Do Yourself a Favor: Forgive!

Forgiveness is the making of a decision to release the offending person and/or situation. It's choosing to let go of resentment, bitterness and our right to get even. Sometimes forgiveness is a process that takes time. It means letting go of the past and its hold on you. As Isaiah 43:18 says "Forget the former things, do not dwell on the past."

Our past wounds can be affecting our relationships today. They may have us bound and stuck in places we are not even aware of. Emotional healing and forgiveness are essential for building healthy relationships and a more enjoyable life.

Decide to forgive your ex-spouse, ex-in-laws, your current spouse and anyone else who has hurt you or your children. Are you harboring bitterness toward God for allowing it to happen to you? How about yourself, do you need to forgive you?

Forgiveness is essential for moving ahead, but so is emotional healing. What happened to you happened! What you do with it today will determine who you are tomorrow.

Emotional wounds are like puncture wounds on the skin. Until that fleshly wound is healed, you are very guarded with it, you won't let anyone touch it and if they do, you pull away from them quickly. Don't allow your emotional wounds to keep you from having the relationships you want—instead, get healed! Don't pull away from your family.

Living in a sin fallen world causes wounds in all of us. But God, in His goodness, has provided for our healing. Exodus 15:26 says, "For I am the Lord who heals you." He is our Healer; physically, mentally, spiritually and emotionally.

Steps Toward Forgiveness and Healing

A simple yet very effective formula to aid you in the process of forgiving and for healing is:

1. Ask God to reveal the wound He wants to heal. You may have buried issues that are hindering you without your even realizing it. Or you may know the area in which you need healing. It's something you have to deal with daily. When God reveals an area in your life that is wounded, it is to heal you. The key is to be as honest with God as you know how. Then commit the situation to Him and trust Him to help you get healed. ***God can do in very little time what could take a counselor many years to do.***

2. Release and give your hurt, pain, wound, fear, anger or frustration to God (be honest with Him about how you feel—He can handle it)! Allow God **in** to your pain, He is gentle and will only heal you. He will **not** leave your wound open and exposed; He will mend it so that the pain is actually gone—if you let Him.

3. Ask God to search your heart and reveal any areas of unforgiveness. David says in Psalm 139: 23,24 "Search me, O

God, and know my heart! Try me, and know my thoughts! And see if there is any wicked or hurtful way in me, and lead me in the way everlasting."

4. Release and forgive others, God, and yourself. Unforgiveness holds you in bondage. Once you've decided to forgive, the healing process can begin. The hurt and anger might not dissolve all at once but you have opened the door for God to come in and heal your heart. Forgiveness is a process that could take some time, especially if you've been deeply wounded. You must confess your own unforgiveness; look at the full impact of your hurt and work through those painful memories. This will bring you to a place of forgiveness and healing. There are no shortcuts. To pretend that you have forgiven when you haven't will only delay your healing. ***Forgive because it's God's will and it's good for <u>you</u>.***

If you believe the offense done against you is too large to forgive, ask God to help you forgive. He does not despise your honesty. Actually, when we are truthful, He is free to work on our behalf. He doesn't require anything from us that He won't enable us to do.

Once you've asked God to help you forgive and you've made the decision to release the offender, feelings of forgiveness will eventually follow. You may not feel them right away but if you continue to stand in forgiveness and refuse to pick back up the offense, you will come to a place where that old wound has lost its sting and power over you. You will be free to be all that God made you to be because "Whom the Son sets free is free indeed." (John 8:36). It is really for your own good that you forgive; it will go well with you and free you to move on.

Repent for hurting others out of your own hurt. Ask the Lord to forgive you for your part. 1st John 1:9, 10 says, "If we confess our sins, He is faithful and just and will forgive us our sins and purify us from all unrighteousness. If we claim we have not sinned, we make Him out to be a liar and His word has no place in our lives."

Ask God to heal the hurt. Give Him time to heal you in whatever way He chooses. Some may cry tears of healing, others may feel a burden lift, yet others may not sense a whole lot going on as they wait on the Lord. But in the days to come when they think about the person or situation that hurt them, the pain and anger will be gone. God will deal with you on an individual basis because He is a personal God.

5. Finally, guard your mind. The enemy will use everyday circumstances to try and bring back the offense or wound that you have forgiven. When this happens, focus on the Lord and praise Him for who He is. Don't give the enemy entrance to your mind. He will try to get you to focus on what happened to you but don't let him. He is a liar and wants to keep you trapped in the past so that you can't move forward.

Healing For All

Matt and Donna have been married for 15 years. Matt was married with four children when he met Donna who had one son out of wedlock. Both were wounded when they met and were searching for significance and wholeness. They were attracted to each other and became emotionally involved.

Matt decided to leave his wife and four kids for the "other woman". Shortly thereafter, however, Donna decided she really didn't want to marry Matt and that decision plunged him into a deep depression. He had lost everything but during that time of hopelessness and despair he found the Lord as his personal Savior.

Matt and Donna did reunite sometime later and were married. Everything seemed to be fine; they were serving the Lord, had purchased a new home and were expecting their first child together. Then his four children came to live with them.

Donna tried to love them but as she puts it "they were animals." They literally destroyed her brand new home. Things were broken that she didn't know could break. She didn't like his children and they didn't like her. After all, she had taken their dad away from their mom and had "caused" their parents to divorce.

Matt's ex-wife, Josie, had remarried, but working together for the good of the kids was out of reach. There was just too much hurt. The four children didn't do well through the years. They were involved in gangs, drugs and one even went to jail.

Donna had very little to do with Matt's ex-wife; she had only seen her once. Obviously, Josie was not anxious to talk to the woman who had helped to tear her family apart. So Matt handled all of the communication with Josie about the children, but that usually didn't go well because there was a lot of hurt and anger between them still.

Then a death occurred in the family and both couples were brought together. Matt's father passed away and since his parents never accepted Donna or his marriage to her, but still considered his first wife to be their daughter-in-law, she attended the funeral.

Josie, her husband Ted, and the four children (who were now living with their mom and step-dad) were there, along with Matt and his family. They were all thrust together for several days whether they liked it or not. But the Lord was up to something good since Josie and Ted had recently accepted Jesus as their Lord and many changes and healings had taken place in their own lives. Now all four adults were serving the Lord and each was willing to forgive and allow God to mend their hearts of the past.

Unquestionably, before Josie had asked the Lord into her life, she had nothing but disdain for Donna. But due to the forgiveness she experienced in her own life from the Lord, she was able to forgive Donna and Matt.

Given that they were all together, it was likely that they would have to communicate on some level with one another. Surprisingly, one day Josie and Donna were found talking to each other for quite awhile about the children and their newfound mutual love for the Lord. They were actually enjoying each other! That began not just a superficial relationship but a friendship that would last and actually benefit the whole family, especially the children.

Sometime later, Matt and Josie's daughter became engaged. The wedding would be in Texas where Josie and her family lived. That meant Matt, Donna, and their children would have to make travel arrangements to attend the wedding. Josie and Ted insisted they stay with them. They actually opened up their home and their hearts to Matt and Donna. They not only made them feel right at home but they served them and provided for their needs. Josie had invited the "other woman" into her home and then went the extra mile by serving her.

Matt and Donna were very humbled by the love and forgiveness they received from Josie and Ted. They were treated with respect and love, though Josie had every right, by human standards, to be bitter and angry. She put that aside, forgave both of them and allowed God to heal her heart of its wounds.

She is a beautiful example of what God can do if we are willing to trust Him and opt to forgive those who have hurt us. She chose to forgive and forget what was behind. She could have focused on the fact that Donna "stole" her husband or that Matt walked out on her and their children, but she chose instead to forgive and look ahead. Because of her decision to forgive and get healed, she is free of the past and is enjoying the present.

Forgiveness is a decision and sometimes it can only be made with much pain because oftentimes we feel we are justified in **not** forgiving and in holding onto bitterness. God never said to forgive except in the case of _____ (fill in the blank). No, He simply says to forgive 77 times (Matthew 18:22). Seven is the number of completeness, so we must completely forgive every time someone hurts us.

Amazingly, the two families are good friends today. They have teamed up to help their children and today the children are all doing well. Each one is serving the Lord and making good choices. Because forgiveness was granted, everyone has benefited.

Donna conveyed her story with love and admiration for her husband's ex-wife. There is no bitterness between the two families and she actually told what happened in a way so as to make Josie a hero by the way she released the past and forgave.

The Bible says satan comes to kill, steal, and destroy whatever he can of ours. But God is greater. When we commit our situation to Him, and do what is required of us (like forgiving), He can turn the whole mess around.

Only God can heal a woman to the place that she can invite her adulterer ex-husband and his new wife into her home and then trust them to be her friends. Josie is a wise woman who chose to forgive. This released her to live a much fuller and richer life.

When we follow the principals of forgiveness and open ourselves up to receive healing, we are free to move on. The past cannot hold us back.

Spotlight on my Emotions

Instant Replay: Forgiving and allowing for my emotional wounds to be healed are essential for moving on to greater freedom and happiness.

Self Examination: Is there anyone in my life who I have not forgiven? Do I have wounds that are holding me back?

Action: Identify the emotional wounds that are hindering my relationships and me. I will follow the steps toward forgiveness and healing and get free of the past!

Chapter 4

Highway to Intimacy

"...There is a friend who sticks closer than a brother."
Proverbs 18:24b

First marriages have the ideal set-up. There are no children yet, so there is the opportunity for the couple to cleave to each other without interference from other relationships. This gives them a chance to foster uninterrupted intimacy.

In a healthy family, the primary and most important relationship is the marriage. The bond between a husband and wife must be strong, united, and first. They must cleave to each other, which actually means to cling together.

This process of cleaving could be hindered if the couple must focus their attention on child rearing. When a couple marries with children, cleaving must take place between the couple, and bonding must take place not only between the couple, but also with the children and between the stepsiblings. This requires work and commitment.

Establishing Healthy Bonds

When a person remarries with children, most likely there is already a bond established between the parent and child that is strong. Not so with the stepparent. Since this is different from God's original order because He intended for the couple to bond first and then bring children into the family, problems could arise. So when a marriage partner steps into an already made family and naturally tries to cleave to his partner; jealousies, competition, and loyalty issues can surface.

It can be painful for the child to allow another person to come into his "already made family" and assume the important role of "spouse" to his or her parent. If it's a son who lived alone with his mom, he has been the "man of the house." It's not an easy thing to give up that role and title to another. It means stepping down from a role he's grown accustomed to (even if this title is not spoken, the boy often assumes it because it is built into him to protect the women in his life including his mom). If it's a girl who lives with her daddy, she must step down from her place as the "woman of the house" and allow her stepmother to have it. It is not a simple feat for any girl, no matter what her age, to take a second seat in position to the man in her life.

When you have a child who is struggling to accept your spouse and the new family unit, it makes it harder for you to cleave to your spouse and put him first. Naturally, you want to help your child and comfort him. You want to assure him that he is still as important to you as before the marriage and sometimes you feel like you have to prove this point. When a parent is busy convincing a child that she still loves him as much as before, it takes time and energy away from bonding with a spouse and stepchildren.

According to Dr. Randy Carlson, Family Counselor, children who are raised by interested, biological parents usually do better than those who are raised by a single parent or a parent and a stepparent. Adults often see remarriage as a second chance but their children don't always see it that way. Stepchildren are twice as likely to have behavioral problems as children raised in the nuclear home with their own mom and dad. This acting out could be due to anger over the divorce and what it has meant to them. It could be from fear and insecurities about the future. Stepfamilies have been called the most volatile family form in America. Many stepfamilies divorce (over half) due to the problems that arise because of the "step" situation.

In light of this, bonding with your spouse and stepchildren is critical to making your new family work. But it won't just happen; you have to **make it happen.**

Some Ways to Encourage the Bonding Process

- For the first year or two of your marriage, minimize your outside commitments. Commit as much time to your new family as possible.
- Have dates with your spouse; having time alone should be a priority.
- Have dates with the kids, both step and natural. You need to get to know your stepchildren on a one-to-one basis but your natural child also needs to have special time alone with you.
- Have family night. Play games, go for a walk or to the park, do something together that you all enjoy.
- Watch videos of your stepchildren when they were babies on up to the age where you came into their life. Watch them together and tell them how cute they are. This will help you to bond with them, and then, when times get difficult you will have a memory bank built from which to draw from.
- One night per week, one child gets to pick out his favorite dish for dinner. He will have a special place setting

with a special glass to signify that it is his "special night." After a fun dinner of talking and sharing, the rest of the family must say something positive to that child. Maybe something they like about him or something they did for him. Each person must build that child up so when he leaves the table, he feels like a million bucks. Also, he doesn't have to help with the dishes that night! Having to say something nice to that person causes the family to focus on his good qualities, not the bad, thus helping the bonding process.

- Try to give equal time to the children so that jealousy and competition will not arise.
- Go to the children's games together and cheer them on.
- Make getting to know each member of your family a priority.
- Don't be lazy about *fostering the bonding process*. I can say from experience that you will not feel like putting the energy into doing it at times. Make it a commitment and your reward will be great.

Rely on the God of Hope

Though the child of a blended family might have a tougher road, if you, the parents, will join together to do what is right by them, in the end they will flourish. That means they will blossom, thrive, succeed and prosper.

We have four children with three of them being in a step situation. The three are grown now and I can tell you it wasn't easy. Each one of them went through some sort of behavioral difficulty in their teen years. Though my husband and I made many mistakes, we were diligent about trying to raise our family according to the Word of God. He has been faithful to restore and redeem every situation.

Each of our children agree that they are the people they are today because of their blended family experience. We held our children accountable for their own actions, disciplined when necessary and tried to show each one they were important and loved by God and us.

Though our children may have suffered from our poor choices of the past, if you choose to live according to God's principals today, He will turn it all out for good as He did for our family. Make every effort to bond with your family. Commit each relationship and situation to Him; He will take care of the rest.

I used to feel that my marriage was not the best for my son. Now that he is an adult and flourishing, I am convinced it was. My husband and son were iron sharpening iron and God used our family to turn a boy into a man.

My husband taught him things I never could. He required things of him that I never would. He modeled being a husband and father; he did not baby him, but helped him to grow into a man. Today, I realize the profound and positive impact my husband had on our son and am so thankful for his fatherly role in his life. I know our son would not be the man he is today if he hadn't had his stepfather's influence. They had a rocky and oftentimes antagonistic relationship when he was younger, but today they respect each other and are developing a friendship that will last for eternity.

A High Calling

When you find yourself in a step situation, take comfort in the fact that God has trusted you to raise another person's child. He sees something in you that you can impart to a child you did not conceive. Thank Him for the responsibility but also remind Him that you are in need of His daily help and grace to be a loving parent to your stepchild.

The relationships in a blended situation are unique and can be all tied up and complex. But they are workable and can be successful if we choose to operate in the right attitude. We must decide to serve others in love. Jesus himself said in John 13:34,35 "A new command I give you: Love one another. As I have loved you so you must love one another. By this all men will know that you are my disciples, if you love one another." There is no higher calling than to be a disciple (follower) of Christ and He says that by our love, others will know we belong to Him.

Realize that though you may not like someone in your family, you **are** required to love them. You are accountable to do what is right by them and to respect them. You cannot abuse them in any way, not physically, verbally, or emotionally. As the adults of the family, you are accountable to God about how you handle your relationships. Did you lean on God for help and guidance? Did you seek outside help if the problem was too big to handle alone? Did you ask God to give you His heart toward the step-member you are having so much difficulty with? Are you praying for him or her regularly? You can't harbor bitterness toward someone you pray for earnestly; eventually God's love for that person will come into your heart.

As the adults in the family, we are held accountable for what we know and how we act on that information. It's not enough to know what is right—we must do it. Bonding occurs automatically in a "typical" family. The husband and wife spend time together alone and hopefully develop a level of intimacy before any children come along. Then, when the children do come along, and this is the baby you conceived together, and planned and looked forward to together, then bonding comes easily with your child. However, in a blended family, you not only have to bond with your spouse, but you also have to bond and get to know the children too. These are children you didn't conceive, you didn't see them take their first steps or hear their first words. And now you are a parent to them.

Bonding will only happen if the family is willing to work at it. Time, attention, and energy must be given to each new relationship for it to obtain a measure of bonding and intimacy. When you are bonded, there will be a feeling of being connected to one another and a sense of closeness. As the parents, make the effort to connect with your new family. Do what you know is right even though the children might not respond to you the way you would like them to. They may not even accept you until later in life. This was Ed and Jill's experience.

Finally, the Reward!

They each had a son from their previous marriage. Ed's son, John, was nine when they married and Jill's son, Mark, was seven. John was strong-willed and used to having his own way.

Ed is a fireman who was gone much of the time and left John to stay with Grandma and Grandpa who did very little disciplining. John pretty much ran the show and got what he wanted. Ed was rather lenient as a parent due to feelings of guilt over the divorce and having to leave his son so much of the time.

John had wanted to live with his mother and sister but his mom said she just couldn't allow that since he was such a difficult child. This hurt John deeply causing him to feel rejected by her so he dealt with it by lashing out in anger. But not toward his mom—instead his anger was directed at his dad and step mom. This often happens—the child *will lash out at the ones with whom they feel the most secure*. Mark, Jill's son, on the other hand, was a pleaser and a joy to have around. He was very easy to get along with; he was obedient and rarely caused a problem. And so they had two sons, each on the opposite end of the spectrum.

Before their marriage, everyone told Jill how good she would be for John. She would be the one to help get him under control. Her life's vocation includes working with children so she understands them and can usually win their love and respect. Not so with John, at least not while he was living with them. Jill says she tried everything she knew to win him, but nothing worked. Bonding and a feeling of closeness just never happened for this blended family. The boys never connected because they were so different.

Jill and Mark enjoyed a loving mother-son relationship but so much of Jill's time and attention was focused on John and that caused Mark to have feelings of being left out and unimportant. Mark required very little discipline but it seemed like there was some sort of crisis with John every day.

Even mealtimes were nothing to look forward to because John had developed an eating disorder. He was attempting to regain, unconsciously through inappropriate eating, some of the control he felt he had lost when Jill married his father. So John was disruptive during mealtime which could have been a time of enjoyment and bonding. Instead it became something to dread.

It felt like the whole family revolved around John. Jill spent most of her time disciplining, training, and dealing with John's behavior while her son felt left out and ignored. Ed was gone much of the time but when he was home, they spent their time dealing with John. John was not only preventing any bonding from taking place between himself and others but also between other family members. I don't want to paint a picture that John was a bad child. He wasn't. But he was a hurt child. Many times hurting people lash out to hurt others, and will erect protective walls, so no one can penetrate and hurt them again.

When Jill was asked why she hung in with Ed who was gone so much of the time and which left her to deal with his child who was very vocal about his feelings toward her, she responded with "I promised myself I wouldn't get another divorce and I knew one day the boys would be gone and it would be Ed and me." They were committed to the marriage regardless of the difficult the situation.

All parents want to believe the best about their own children. They want to believe they are just as intelligent, just as obedient, and just as loving as any other child. When it became evident to all that there were behavioral differences between the boys, Ed became resentful toward Mark because he "outshone" his son. Consequently, he began looking for things that Mark didn't do right.

His defensiveness about his own son caused him to look for things in Mark that would cause his disapproval. Each child must be dealt with on an individual basis. Disciplining one because of the behavior of another will prove to be very harmful to everyone involved.

John left the home at the age of 17 and when he left, he really left. His parents didn't hear from him for over two years. They didn't know at times whether he was dead or alive. Then, one day when John was 20, a friend of Jill's told her that she had received an invitation to his wedding. Ed and Jill had not been invited and they had never even met his fiancé. They, of course, wanted to go, so they prayed about it and then phoned John to ask if they could come. He said they could, but since "Jill is not my mother she cannot sit at the head table with us." Ed chose not to sit at the head table either; instead he sat with his wife.

Several years have passed since the wedding. John has children of his own now and his eyes have been opened to many things he didn't understand when he was younger. He now refers to Jill as "Mom" and checks in with her regularly. He is raising his children the way his parents tried to raise him, with healthy authority and respect. His relationship with his family has been restored. They have a level of intimacy and bonding that they enjoy today *but the foundation for it was laid when the kids were in the home.*

Though John pushed Jill away while he was in her home, she continued to be involved in his life. Her involvement was usually met with resistance, but Ed and Jill worked hard to do what was right by their boys even though there were things working against them. If just one thing could have been different, such as Ed being able to come home each night, perhaps his son would have been less angry and bonding could have occurred more quickly for all of them. But the point is that bonding did take place.

They didn't give up when their family life was unhappy, they hung in there and now they are reaping the rewards. Children may reject you and your efforts while they're in your home. But, many times when they move out they begin to realize the sacrifice and commitment you gave them, and they want to "come back" and have that close relationship with you.

Created for Intimacy

Intimacy is something that is developed and maintained. It's not something that once it develops is there for the rest of your relationship. It's something that has to be nurtured and cared for. It's a feeling of closeness and the ability to share the most private and personal parts of yourself and it must be coupled with trust. You can't be intimate with someone if you don't trust him or her. You wouldn't share secrets with someone you fear would use your secrets against you as a weapon.

Intimacy is an inborn need we all have. We need to have someone to confide in, someone to share our heart's desires with and our hopes, dreams and fears. We all need to feel connected to someone and know we are accepted just the way we are. The Lord desires an intimate relationship with His children; this is one main reason why He created us.

He offered intimacy to the nation of Israel in the Old Testament but they refused His offer. After all He had done for them by bringing them out of Egypt, keeping them in the desert and guiding them along their way, they still did not desire to have an intimate relationship with Him. They told Moses to "go near and listen to all that the Lord our God says. Then tell us whatever the Lord our God tells you. We will listen and obey."

(Deuteronomy 5:27). They were not interested in a personal relationship with the Lord themselves so they could hear His voice individually. Instead they wanted Moses to be close to Him and then tell them what He said.

The reason the Israelites were not interested in a personal, intimate relationship with God is because they did not understand Him. They knew He was powerful and mighty but they did not know Him as a Father. They knew He could do the impossible and that He expected certain behaviors from them, but they did not know His heart. God even tried to talk to them so they could hear His voice for themselves, but they refused the closeness of the relationship. Because God's chosen people would not allow intimacy and fellowship with Him, their commitment and what love they had for Him eventually became very weak.

Any relationship that is to be close, including one between God and His people, husband and wife, parent and child, needs communication with understanding, intimacy and knowledge of one another's heart. We cannot expect to obtain a level of intimacy unless all parties are willing to get to know the other and unveil themselves. God was willing to unveil Himself to these people, but they were afraid because they didn't choose to understand God, thus denying the relationship and instead accepting a set of rules and regulations (the Ten Commandments and the Books of the Law).

Sometimes anger, fear, or erected walls can get in the way of intimacy and bonding to occur. If this is the case in your family, talk it out or seek counseling. Get to the root of the problem and deal with it so you can move on into a closer and more fulfilling and workable relationship. *Your relationship is worth the time and effort. Don't throw it away because you don't understand each other.*

The Israelites refused a relationship with the living God, and of course eventually didn't obey His commands either (rules without a relationship=rebellion). They rebelled against God and His laws even though they were the ones who rejected the relationship. But God in His great love for mankind sent His son to be the perfect sacrifice so that we humans could enter into an intimate relationship with the Creator of all things. God the Father loved His creation, "man," so much that He was willing to have His own perfect Son die for us so that we could enter into relationship with Him. Even though man had rejected a relationship with Him at first, that didn't prevent the Father from finding another way.

Jesus said He was going to the cross for the "joy set before Him" (Hebrews 12:2). What is that joy? A relationship with us, imperfect man! Is that incredible or what? God couldn't gain the relationship with man that He desired through rules so He went to the extreme to obtain it. We have a wonderful Father who is very interested in each one of us. Notice that God the Father pursued the relationship. Though it originally failed because of our sinful, selfish nature, He continued to do what He could to obtain a relationship with us. He stopped at nothing, even the sacrificing of His own dear Son.

Steps Toward Intimacy

By learning from God and how He obtained intimacy with those who will enjoy it with Him, we can use these same steps in fostering closer relationships in our own family.

The first is to **pursue** your relationship. It will not just happen. You must put effort into it and you must decide whether that particular relationship is worth your time. The third listing in Webster's Dictionary for pursue is to try to find, strive for, seek. These are action words with a purpose in mind, to seek to know the person you are pursuing

The next step is to **understand** the people you with whom you want to bond. Try to understand them as a person, look inwardly at their heart not at their external behavior or appearance. Sometimes the ones who seem the hardest or most aloof are the ones who need you the most.

The third step is to **communicate** openly and honestly. Even if it is hard, let them know you would like a relationship with them. Tell them they are valuable to you, this could break down the walls they've erected and a true relationship could begin to develop. Communicate through your actions. Make sure your actions line up with your words. Actions speak louder than words.

Respect your family members. They deserve this simply because they are made in God's image. You must respect others to receive it.

Model God's character and His ways. We are the parents and our children are learning from us. Model for them God's way, not the world's. Teach them to love and serve others, not to just look out for "Number One."

These steps are ongoing. You can't just do them once and think you've obtained intimacy. You haven't; they must be practiced over and over again. If, as the joke goes, you told your spouse only once that you love him or her and never said affirming words again, your relationship would deteriorate. It couldn't grow without an honest effort of pursuing, understanding, communicating, respecting and modeling.

Respect is a very important key to developing a healthy relationship and maintaining it. We all have a basic need to be respected; even children have this need. To gain respect, you must give respect. Don't overstep your boundaries; don't force relationships with step members if they aren't quite ready for it. Gently let them know you are available to them and love them regardless of how they feel about you at the time.

Modeling Love

Teryl had a choice to make. Her husband's eldest son wanted nothing to do with her. He had moved out of their home shortly after they wed because he never wanted them to get married. He dealt with it by excluding himself from the family.

Teryl knew she had to do something. She couldn't allow her husband's son to eliminate himself from the family on account of her. So every so often, Teryl would write him a letter inviting him to come over. In the letter, she would say how much they all missed him and could he please come to dinner. She also suggested he bring his laundry to do at their home.

Eventually he realized Teryl wasn't the enemy and even began to acknowledge her as his father's wife. Had she not taken the time to pursue him, understand his feelings (and not take offense), communicate her desire to have a relationship, respect him and model Christ, a relationship would never have developed between them.

Choosing God's Way

In a stepfamily, you will have diverse relationships develop and from these several unique situations will arise. From divided loyalties to standoff aloofness, to angry, hateful or indifferent attitudes all the way to accepting and loving relationships—in one family, you could experience the whole gamut on the relational spectrum. Regardless of how others in your family are choosing to behave, you can take the first step and choose to behave according to God's Word. The choice is yours, but the rewards will be great if you choose God's way.

Spotlight on my Relationships

Instant Replay: Cleaving, bonding and intimacy require extra work in a blended family but it's worth the effort.

Self Examination: In what ways am I initiating and fostering the bonding process in my family? Am I developing intimacy through pursuing, understanding, communicating, respecting and modeling Christ to the one I would like to connect with?

Action: This week I will initiate family time and try to make it at a time when the whole family can participate. I will have a date with one member of my family who needs it the most.

Chapter 5

Will This Ride Ever End? Our Story

"Let us hold unswervingly to the hope we profess, for He who promised is faithful."   *Hebrews 10:23*

One scripture I've hung onto over the years is found in Genesis 18:14 and it asks the question: "Is anything too hard for the Lord?" In the midst of strife, anger and jealousies my answer is always "No, there is nothing too difficult for my God."

He can bring order out of chaos, exchange peace for strife, love for jealousy, compassion for anger, and He can even cause two separate families, with all their own intricate workings, to blend and live in harmony. You might be thinking, "Not this family of mine! We have people who don't like each other, and we have the strong willed and those who are just plain hard to get along with. Sometimes it feels like World War Three has erupted right in our home!" I know what you mean, because at times it felt like we were in the middle of a great war that would never end.

After the Honeymoon

The strife in our home began a few years after we were married. We had many obstacles and differences to overcome. My husband Ron is from Australia and I am an American which results in cultural differences. We were both married to our first spouses for about 5 years; we had that in common as well as our love for the Lord. Ron has been a controller and I have been a pleaser although we are now working to stop these unhealthy behaviors as they are not conducive to a good relationship.

He has a daughter from his first marriage and I have a son from mine. They are both blonde but that's about the extent of what they have in common except for the fact that they both know the pain from the breakup of their family. As you can see, we had a lot of "blending" to do as even our cultures are different. Our own experiences growing up in different countries added to the strife because each of us thought the way our culture did it was right so that's how we should raise our family.

After a 10 month whirlwind romance, we were married. We were very much in love and believed it was God's will for us to bring our families together in holy matrimony. We had a few sessions of marriage counseling but the issues of a blended family were never brought up.

We didn't realize going into our marriage that second families have issues to face that first marriages do not have. Problems such as manipulations and interferences from ex-spouses and their families, lack of love and acceptance between stepparent and stepchild, when and how the stepparent should implement discipline toward the stepchild and the problem of a biological parent who could be overly focused on her own child (thus leaving the new spouse or stepchild out), or the problem of a stepparent who is too harsh.

At first, our family consisted of us, yours, and mine. We were doing fairly well considering the great strains that visitations would cause. Our son, Keenan, age six, would visit his dad where, it seemed, many of the rules that we considered important, did not apply in his dads home. Values in each home were different so Keenan would have to adjust and readjust over and over again.

My son was told that my new husband was not his dad and that he didn't have to do anything he said. My husband was called ugly names in my son's presence, making any type of bonding very difficult. Keenan already knew that Ron was not his dad, but the continual defaming of him made it hard for Keenan to accept him even as his mom's husband. He felt disloyal to his own father if he liked or even enjoyed his step dad.

Shari, Ron's daughter, was seven at the time of our marriage. She lived with her mother who had threatened that she would never allow Shari to have a relationship with her father. She did what she could to keep her promise. Visitations were very difficult. Shari felt like she was betraying her mother if she loved us or had fun with us. She eventually cut herself off from us emotionally because of the guilt she felt from her mother for loving us and wanting to see us.

Because we lived in the same city as both of our exes, and due to the high level of stress it caused, we decided to move out of state. And so, close to two years after we were married, we moved to California because we both love the ocean. We chose to preserve our marriage and our family unit by eliminating some of the incredible outside stresses being near our exes created.

God blessed us with an "ours" two and a half years after we were married. We bought our first home, a fixer-upper, two years after her birth. Most weekends were spent working on our new home and the stresses of everyday life were mounting.

I began to notice a real pattern in Ron, who at that time was a controller. Keenan had certain chores to do Saturday morning before he could go play. Invariably, he did something "wrong."

47

This would start the three of us (Ron, myself and Keenan) off on the wrong foot for the whole weekend. Ron would get angry with Keenan and punish him harshly. I would jump in (the pleaser) and try to smooth over the situation, only to make it worse. The three of us were in a tightly woven web that was weakening our relationships.

Let me paint the picture: Keenan would awaken Saturday morning excited that it was the weekend and he'd have a good part of the day to play with his friends, once his chores were done. He was very energetic and active and loved to go outdoors. Because Ron and I were not communicating well at the time, particularly about how to discipline our kids, there was no agreement as to what discipline would be appropriate for what offense. We just flew by the seat of our pants and that caused much disunity, anger and strife.

Keenan, eager to go play, would sometimes miss doing a part of a chore in the backyard. Then Ron would go in the backyard to work on a project only to find the job unfinished. Keenan would be called back to finish his work but invariably a bomb would go off. Anger and hot tempers would fly and the next thing that would come out of Ron's mouth is "And you're grounded for the whole weekend."

Well, I felt my little cub was being treated unfairly, so in steps Mama Bear. Then Mama and Papa would go round and round while Baby Bear sat in his room. This was an unhealthy situation for all of us including Chelsea, the "ours." Family days were getting more and more strained and it seemed that peace was out of reach for our family.

We were going through stages in the Blending process that we did not understand nor had we ever heard of. We were stuck somewhere between the grind, stir and the puree buttons. At times we felt like ground beef being crushed into bits. At other times, we were like iron sharpening iron. Yet, at other times, we just felt like mush and wondered if it was really worth going on together. We found out that it was worth going on together because eventually we reached the "mix" and "blend" buttons.

The cycle I spoke of earlier occurred for many years in our family. It wasn't until Keenan was in his teen years and the three of us had gone in for counseling that one of the causes of this merry-go-round was revealed. Before I met Ron, it was Keenan and me. We were very close and enjoyed each other immeasurably. We were living with my mom at the time, which we all enjoyed, but I told Keenan that one day we were going to buy our own home, just the two of us. Well, my little 5 year-old took that to heart and looked forward to us obtaining a new home one day, just his and mine.

Then I met and fell in love with Ron and 10 short months later we had a new home, just the three of us. Keenan never mentioned that he didn't like Ron in our family but Ron sensed his rejection. The more Ron felt his rejection, the stricter and harsher he became. He was going to get respect one way or another.

Also, Ron is a firm disciplinarian. We had no clue that for the first year, at least, of a blended family, the natural parent should do the disciplining while the stepparent builds a relationship with his/her new child. We didn't do that! Ron was now the head of the house and I was willing to let him step in as a father with all the discipline rights that come with that role.

Ron and I never took the time after that horrible cycle began to discuss a better way to handle disciplining Keenan. That was the thing we argued about, but the real issue was lack of communication in our marriage. I was such a pleaser that I didn't want to bring up anything that could cause friction between us when there was peace. Ron controlled through anger. He would want things done his way and there was little room for disagreement or another opinion, not even mine. He saw me as taking Keenan's side so he was unwilling to hear what I had to say. Keenan saw me as taking Ron's side so he had built up anger towards me. I, the Pleaser, could not please either one.

We did not get victory from this merry-go-round until God stepped in through a counselor who saw what each of us was doing and explained the whole mess to us. Once we saw it, we repented for our own part in it and asked each other for forgiveness. We asked God to forgive us and asked Him to help us change.

We had to be willing to repent, change, and forgive. These three steps are key. If just one of us had acknowledged our own part in the cycle, we could have broken the pattern. Don't wait for your partner to change, even if he is a large part of the problem—you must change! Don't participate in unhealthy responses any more. Get to the root of the problem and deal with it. If it is a lack of communication in your marriage, get help so you can talk.

Rewards of Sacrifice

When Keenan was 14 and Chelsea was 5, my brother, who was a single parent, died, leaving his only son to come and live with us. We were in the midst of trying to "blend" ourselves when we brought "Theirs" into our home. Nelson was 10 years old when his father died. It had been the two of them since Nelson was a year old when his parents had divorced. Nelson has two half brothers from his mother's first marriage but he was raised an only child until he became a part of our family.

In our house, Nelson and Keenan would have to share a room. This was a new thing for both of them since they had always had their own rooms. Keenan was "a tidy" and Nelson was "a messy." They had some adjustments to make, but Nelson had to make some major adjustments. He had to make his bed daily, clean up after himself, and put things away. If he didn't, Keenan would be all over him. I didn't have to say much to Nelson because Keenan made sure he cleaned up after himself. Consequently Nelson went from being messy to being fairly clean.

My brother died the day after Christmas, in another state. Nelson had lived in the same neighborhood all of his life and had attended just one elementary school where he did very well. January came and he now lived in a new state, with a new family and a new school. He was mourning the loss of his father, his home, his friends, and everything he knew. He felt abandoned and rejected by his mother who did not bring him to live with her. We tried school for a few weeks but he did not do well at all. He didn't know anyone and didn't much care to. He daydreamed a lot and found it very challenging to even concentrate. The Lord prompted me to home school him so that our bond could become stronger and help him through this very difficult period of his life. So I gave up all of my activities and outside ministries to home school the newest member of our family.

This commitment was not easy for me. Our youngest had just started school and I finally had some time for myself to pursue some personal interests. The Lord asked me to give them up for the time being so I could bond with Nelson and become his mom.

Those months were a time when my flesh, and everything I wanted, had to die. I needed to be available to a little boy who desperately needed care and attention. He had been diagnosed Attention-Deficit Hyperactivity Disorder (ADHD) but we refused to put him on Ritalin as the doctors had suggested. He was very hyperactive, and for the first time in my life I knew what it was like to have my noise toleration level invaded. The noise level in our home went up so dramatically that it felt like 10 people had moved in, not one. I remember going into my bathroom to get away from the noise and to be alone with the Lord for a few moments. But invariably, Nelson would stand outside my door knocking and waiting for me to come out.

Many evenings, by the time my husband got home, I was in tears and needed him to take over (which he did very graciously). Nelson was a very high maintenance child. He needed so much emotional and physical attention that, by the time my other children got home from school, there was little of me left to devote to them. Needless to say, this was a very difficult and strenuous time for our family. Would we do it differently today? No way. God was very faithful to carry us all the way through. Children are worth investing in.

Establishing a United Front

Ron and I always had dates with time for just the two of us, but something was missing: true communication. We shared the day's events with each other and enjoyed each other's company, but talking on a deep and intimate level was rare.

We didn't know how to express ourselves when something bothered us, so we buried it. But it always came up somehow, maybe in anger toward each other or by treating one of the kids inappropriately or harshly. Or if there was already too much chaos going on in the family, we would just shut each other out. Not very effective ways for handling our problems! And on top of that, we were Christians and thought that meant we should be able to handle all of our problems alone, with God's help, and shouldn't need any outside help. So we usually didn't get any.

Had we realized that by having a third party present who was neutral while we discussed issues that were too difficult for us to talk about by ourselves, we could have conquered and abated many issues before they had a chance to grow into real problems. We have learned that many parenting problems can be solved quickly if the parents are communicating and united.

It is important to the whole family that you work first on your marriage and have open and honest communication. The children need to see your united front; it could ward off many of their wayward notions before they have a chance to become a full-blown problem, pattern, or cycle. When the family knows the marriage is first, the other relationships seem to work better as well. The children may try for a while to come in-between you, but will soon give up if they don't find an inroad.

When Nelson came to live with us, our 14-year-old son Keenan, who now had to share his room with a 10-year-old "little kid" struggled quite a bit. He not only had to share his mom with his stepdad and the baby they had together, but now he had to share her with a kid who was loud and took so much of her time. He realized the situation Nelson found himself in was quite devastating so he resolved not to resent him too much for invading his home.

They never really became very close until they no longer lived together in the same house as brothers. Today, however, they are good friends. Chelsea was thrilled when Nelson moved in because she had always had a "crush" on him and now he would be her brother! They had a great relationship through the years; they always had time for each other, played well together and were always pals.

Building Children's Self-Esteem

Ron and I decided we would go on individual dates with each of the children so as to have quality personal time with them. These proved to help our family immensely. The children felt special when their turn came and looked forward to each date. We rarely did anything expensive, maybe go out to lunch, go on a walk, or play a sport or game they liked to play. It was just quality time, doing something they enjoyed and being available to talk about anything and everything that was in their heart and mind. Setting aside individual time for each child makes him/her feel important and special, that they are valuable and worth your time. That is an invaluable gift a parent can give to a child. It builds self-esteem and the benefits your child receives from this simple act can last a lifetime.

Another plan we executed, as mentioned earlier, was to have one child per week have a special night. This meant that he got to decide what Mom cooked for dinner and received a special table setting. The rest of us made it special; it was a night that child received accolades for being the person he is. If he had done something nice or gone out of his way for someone else, we would retell the story so that everyone could hear it and then congratulate and praise him for his act of kindness. Or we would describe a character trait that we particularly appreciate about him. Our words had to be very complimentary, encouraging and uplifting. This proved helpful in bonding our family unit as well because it forced us to look at and think about the positive attributes of each member of our family.

Something that I wish we had done is to have regular family meetings. Families who have implemented these have found a way to work through issues in a healthy way. The recommendation is to set them up regularly and in advance so everyone knows which night of the week the meeting occurs (or month—however often you feel your family would benefit from them). Second, lay down the ground rules before you start the meetings. Some rules might be that family members can express whatever is in their heart and mind but they must do so with respect; there can be no name calling and everyone must wait to speak until the one talking is finished—in other words, no interrupting the person talking.

Communication is key to a healthy and thriving family. This is one tool that can help foster open, honest, and respectful sharing so that all family members have a forum in which to express themselves and talk about what concerns them. This wards off resentment, misunderstandings, and anger that can build up and cause further problems.

Love Never Gives Up

Our visitations with Shari through the years were sparse and far between. Phone calls were rarely forwarded to her so there was little contact. Ron continued to try to develop a relationship and keep the lines of communication open with her but was met with one roadblock after another. The message did get through, however, that we were there for her and so, at the age of 18, she declared that she was going to visit her dad. She came and came again and at the age of 20, after the break-up of a serious, two-year relationship with her boyfriend, she came to live with us. She was in such pain and heartache over the breakup that she cried out to God for help and felt Him tell her to go live with her dad.

God had heard our prayers through the years and now He was sending her to us in HIS TIME. He redeems every situation that is committed to Him; He is amazing for that truly was a miracle! She had been programmed from a young child that she didn't need us nor should she love us and she was told that we did not love her.

Our lives were stressed to the max when Ron left to bring Shari back to live with us. We were both working full-time and we had been told by our landlords that they were moving back into their home so that meant we had to move out (we rented a larger home sometime after Nelson came to live with us). There was little available in the housing market and time was running out.

Finally, two weeks before we were to be out, God literally showed Ron the home we were to buy. Our realtor hadn't shown it to us because it had an exclusive listing and was not in the Multiple Listings Book. It was vacant, which was a requirement now, since we had little time left before needing to be out.. The home had already received a full price offer but the owner had refused it (something about her not liking the way they went about putting in the offer). So the Lord was faithful to us by providing us with a beautiful yet vacant home. We moved in

Thanksgiving weekend, one week after Shari had come to live with us.

As thrilled as we were, we knew that whenever a new member is introduced to the family there will be strains and adjustments and personality clashes. None of us really knew Shari because our time together had been minimal, so naturally we went through a honeymoon period enjoying getting to know one another. We were settling in, but soon began to grate on each others nerves. I now had another female in my home who sometimes acted like a woman and sometimes acted like a little girl. She wanted all the freedoms of a woman but she wanted to be treated like a little girl by her daddy. She would crawl into our bed between us and want to talk like she was eight years old. Of course, she and her dad were making up for lost time, but I had an almost stranger in my home wanting my husband's attentions and affections. Our daughter, Chelsea, struggled with this as well. She was used to being Daddy's only little girl but now she too had to share.

After the honeymoon period, it was a pretty rocky road for a while. There were some deep-seated emotional wounds and hurts that needed to surface and be healed in Shari. She became engaged to a fine young Christian man she met shortly after coming to live with us. They originally were to be married in July of 2000 but ended up resetting the date for one year later. That year proved to be a time of healing and bonding for Shari and us. We were working through things that might never have come up had she married earlier. We reached the Blending Stage that year—something that never would have been accomplished had she not been living with us.

Now, for the first time in our married life, Ron and I have just one child at home, Chelsea, the "Ours." Our home is a place of peace and love and our older children come home frequently which only adds to our lives. Ron and I have said many times that if we hadn't had the Lord to cling to and a strong commitment to our marriage, we would have divorced. We are so blessed today that we hung in there through those very difficult years because God is faithful to reward His children when they choose His way over what may be easy at the time.

It has been shown that if couples, who are in great distress this year, hang in there and continue to try to work things out, in a few years from now, they will be happy that they stayed together. I am referring to hanging on during stressful, difficult times, but not necessarily in situations where there is physical violence or heavy substance abuse. In those situations, wise counsel is needed from someone who knows you and your situation to help decide what is best for you and your children. But I do know that God will be faithful to you as He has been to us; so if you're not in a dangerous situation, Hang In There! It's almost certain that you will be glad you did.

Spotlight on My Own Story

Instant Replay: If you do not give up, you can have an encouraging story about how you made it through the difficult years until your family finally reached the "Blended Stage."

Self Examination: What can I do to help us get to the "Blended Stage"? One thing is I will set up a family meeting so we can discuss our feelings about our family.

Action: What cycle has gone on too long and now is the time to do something about it? What action am **I** willing to take to help correct the situation? Remember: Don't wait for the other person to change, do what you can to help the situation.

Chapter 6

Eating What You Speak!

"Reckless words pierce like a sword, but the tongue of the wise brings healing." Proverbs 12:18

Words are very powerful. They are what God used to create the heavens and the earth. Words can actually bring forth life or death to a person or a situation. We've all experienced teasing on a playground where we were made fun of for being fat, clumsy, having a big nose or for something we wore. It made us feel like we wanted to die on the spot, or we got angry and said mean things back.

The old cliché "Sticks and stones may break my bones but words will never hurt me" is a farce. Words can and do hurt. Through our words we can chose to encourage or discourage, bring hope or hopelessness or we can build up or tear down. The choice is ours. What comes out of our mouth is a reflection of what is in our heart.

Choose Words of Life

Let's consider children as we ponder the subject of words. A child who grows up in a home where he is affirmed for who he is, encouraged to do his best and told that he is a winner, will be a winner. He will thrive because he has people who believe in him and are "rooting" for him. Let's take a child, on the other hand, who is told he's stupid and a loser and that he won't amount to much. His "support system" has repeatedly spoken death over him and so consequently he will never reach his full potential.

I can hear what some of you are thinking. "My kid (or spouse) is stupid, he doesn't do anything right and I'm sick of it! Sometimes I think they purposely act this way to get me mad." I've been where you are; I know how it feels and how easy it can be to **justify** your words of "truth" (which are actually words of slander and anger) about someone else.

A person may have a serious problem he needs to deal with but our part is not to nag him about it or bring it up in a belittling way because that only makes it worse. No one ever changed because they were told they are stupid and won't amount to much.

We all need someone who thinks the best of us even when we haven't been our best. We all need someone who believes in us and trusts us to do it better next time. People will not change when they are discouraged, but encouraged.

Words spoken into the atmosphere have power regardless of whether the person you are speaking about hears them or not. I have a personal example of this. Since alcoholism is in both family lines of our oldest son, Keenan, I had always warned him not to even take the first drink of alcohol. Well, when he was in high school, he took the first drink and then another and then another. He was becoming consumed with partying and having a good time. He was on a path of destruction that even some of his football buddies were concerned. He could consume so much alcohol that it scared even the heartiest of the partiers.

But as his mom, I could not accept a future ruined by alcoholism for him and all the junk that goes with it. I began to pray fervently for him out loud. My words were penetrating the atmosphere to bring life back to our son who was on a path headed for destruction. I did not pray the circumstances surrounding what he was doing to himself, instead I spoke to the future and all the good that I believed could be his. I chose to believe that God had a great future in store for him rather than one that was defiled by alcoholism. I spoke that he was a valuable asset to society, doing his part and being a good citizen. I prayed and spoke and believed that Keenan is a mighty man of God and that he will fulfill a wonderful destiny specifically designed for him. I spoke that he is successful in all areas of his life, spiritually, mentally, physically, emotionally, vocationally and relationally.

God had spoken to me that Keenan is a man of great love but, at that time, all I could see was anger and even hate. But I prayed and spoke that he is a man of love. Did I have times when I cried for my son and just wanted him back, and were there times I doubted that he would ever change? Of course! That's when I would call a friend who had been through this with her son and she always gave me wisdom and encouragement to stand and believe God to deliver him.

If you begin to falter in the words you are speaking and want to tell it like it is, call a friend for encouragement. Sometimes, when we don't see changes as soon as we would like, we can grow weary in standing and believing.

It took two years before I saw a change in our son and that came only after he suffered a tragedy. He got a D.U.I. one night, and that was what he needed to change. God can use bad things that happen to us and turn them around to bring a lot of good into our lives.

Faith is the Substance of Things Hoped For

So many of us speak what we see rather than what we would like to see. Did you catch that? Don't speak the problem and the hopelessness of a situation, rather speak what you want to see and eventually, if you don't give up, you will see it. I'm not talking about naming it and claiming it. I'm talking about words spoken by faith in God to bring about His good purposes and plans for you, your child, your spouse's child or your spouse. If you don't know what God's good plan is for you, look it up in His word. There are many promises there for the believer.

Though it took two years for our prayers and words of life to come true in our son's life, they did come true. Proverbs 12:14 says, "From the fruit of his lips a man is filled with good things as surely as the work of his hands rewards him." As I see the fruit of my prayers and positive words spoken over Keenan, I am filled with good things: things such as thankfulness to God for the awesome young man our son is today, for enjoying a great relationship with him, and for watching him live out the fulfilling destiny God has specifically designed for him.

Proverbs 18:21 says, "The tongue has the power of life and death and those who love it will eat its fruit." The second part says, in my own words, that we will eat the fruit of the words we speak. If we have a tendency to speak life we will see life come forth and we will partake of its sustenance but if we **choose** to speak death, we will eat of its fruit, which is destruction.

Our words can actually agree with God and what He says, or they can agree with satan who comes only to kill, steal, and destroy us (John 10:10). Satan loves to use our words to keep us in bondage.

Speak life and hope rather than what you are actually seeing. Am I saying to deny the truth? Of course not, but be careful how you speak about it and to whom.

I underlined the word choose because the words we speak are a choice. No one is making us slander, criticize, gossip or crush another person with the words we speak about him or her. Our bible study teacher taught a lesson on this very subject. She said that if our words are true about another, and we speak their problem over and over, it's as if we are reinforcing it and keeping them in further bondage. She gave the example of her father who was a very proud man. She and her sister spoke that over and over again about their dad. He went to his death a very proud man and now she struggles against pride on a regular basis. It's as if she is reaping what she sowed through her mouth about another individual, dealing with the very same thing that she didn't like to see in her dad. Psalm 64:8 says, "He will turn their own tongues against them..." Be careful what you say about another, even if it's true and you feel justified, because your own words may come back to haunt you.

In a blended family where patterns have been established prior to the marriage, it can be very difficult to blend all the personalities together to make this new family work happily for everyone. When it doesn't, it can be easy to speak against your stepchild or spouse. It's easy to get frustrated with them because they are not doing things the way you like. But, I warn you, guard your words and choose them carefully for your own good and the good of the new family unit.

Instead of complaining, pray what you would like to see take place or pray the changes you would like to see made in a certain individual or relationship. Prayer works to change the individual and situation whereas speaking negative, discouraging words helps to keep the situation bad and keep the person in bondage. Encourage good behavior if you see a family member doing something positive or, in your opinion, right. Tell her/him what a good job they did or how you appreciate them doing what you have asked.

You might be thinking your situation is impossible. You may say, "I could speak life and pray for the next five years and nothing will change." Or "I do pray and try to speak positive things over my stepfamily and situation but nothing ever changes." I want to encourage you not to give up. Your answer might be right around the corner and, if you give up now, you will never see the fruit of your labor come to pass. Be patient and ask God to encourage you and to let you see something good to help you keep going.

Speak to the Dry Bones

In Ezekiel 37, the Spirit of the Lord brought Ezekiel to a valley of dry, dead and lifeless bones. It doesn't get any more dead than this, but God asked Ezekiel if these bones could live. He asked because He wanted to establish whether Ezekiel believed God could raise them from the dead. Ezekiel's response was "Only you know that, Lord." He was saying that only God had the power and authority to give dry bones life and to restore something that once had life but is now dead.

Maybe your relationship with your spouse or children is all but dead. Do you believe God can restore it? Jesus said, "According to your faith will it be done to you." (Matthew 9:29). Just as it was not difficult for Jesus to restore eyesight to blind men, it is not difficult for Him to restore your family and relationships. Do you believe He will? Do you believe He wants to do this for you and your family? Then let that be the confession of your mouth. Don't go around grumbling about how awful your blended family situation is; rather, go around saying that in Christ, you have a great family who loves the Lord *and* one another.

Notice in Ezekiel 37: Verses 4 and 5, the Holy Spirit told Ezekiel to prophesy (which means to speak God's will or the Word) to the bones "I will make breath enter you, and you will come to life. I will attach tendons to you and make flesh come upon you and cover you with skin; I will put breath in you, and you will come to life." Verses 7 and 8 says he was obedient and

"As I was prophesying, there was a noise, a rattling sound, and the bones came together, bone to bone. I looked, and tendons and flesh appeared on them and skin covered them, but there was no breath in them." In the next few verses Ezekiel is told to prophesy "breathe into these slain, that they may live."

And live, they did! Breath not only entered them, but "they came to life and stood up on their feet—a vast army." Ezekiel believed God could bring life and breath back to dried up bones. He didn't say it's impossible for dead lifeless bones to come back to life, he just believed that God could do it and He did. Remember: "According to your faith will it be done to you."

That is what He wants to do for us. Bring us out of the dried-up dead places where we've been living. He doesn't want our families and relationships to be unhappy and in turmoil. He wants to make them alive and fulfilling and you can help by speaking life over your situations, circumstances and relationships. Just as Ezekiel prophesied, you can speak promises from the Bible over your family members and situations and you will see those promises come true: "According to your faith will it be done to you."

Pray God's Word

I encourage you to find scriptures that bring you hope and begin to pray them over your family. One scripture I've prayed for our family is found in Jeremiah 33 beginning at Verse 6. I just insert our family into it and pray something like this: "God will bring health and healing to our family, He will heal us, His people and will let us enjoy abundant peace and security. He will rebuild us and cleanse us from all the sin we've committed against Him and will forgive our sins of rebellion against Him."

If you have a family member who is not serving the Lord, use scripture and say "Lord, I thank you that _____ is serving you and loves you with all of his heart, mind and soul. Thank you that he walks by the Spirit and not the flesh. Thank you that the fruit of the Spirit is evident in his life, the fruit of love, joy, peace, goodness, etc."

As you say these things, your eyes are on the Lord and what He can do, not on your situation. Thus your hope and faith are being built and that gives you the strength to go on.

He wants our blended families happy and living in unity with each other. He doesn't like the friction and strife any more than we do. So, start speaking words of life over your family and watch what happens. Find scriptures that fit your situation and pray them. Don't just try it and then say it doesn't work "hang in there." Remember, I had to pray and speak life over my son for two years. What if I had given up and said, "God isn't going to answer my prayers, so why bother?" Your answer might be right around the corner.

Remember all the dreams and hopes you had when you married and entered into your blended family? You believed it would be happy and that all of you together would make it work. You thought you'd be happier together than had you remained alone. Don't lose sight of that, even though circumstances say the opposite. Hang onto your hope and start speaking life and what you envision for your family. It will happen because God's Word works. "Life and death are in the power of the tongue," so speak life and hope and the things you want for your family.

You can make a **decision** right now to determine to speak good things into the bad you are facing. You can also decide to speak what you'd like to see happen rather than what you are currently seeing. And then you can trust God to let you eat the good fruit of the words you've been speaking.

Spotlight on My Words

Instant Replay: Words are powerful. They can bring forth life or death, encouragement or discouragement, hope or despair. They can be used to build up or tear down.

Self Examination: My influence over my family is great. Am I choosing to speak words that will help them or hinder them?

Action: I will choose scriptures that pertain to my situation and use them to speak life and hope into my bad relationships or situation. I will guard my tongue so that it will be used for good and not evil.

Chapter 7

Discipline With Teaching in Mind

"No discipline seems pleasant at the time, but painful. Later on, however, it produces a harvest of righteousness and peace for those who have been trained by it." *Hebrews 12:11*

What image comes to your mind when you hear the word discipline? Do you think of anger, trouble, punishment, rage or unfairness? Or do you imagine teaching and training? **How** you think of discipline is how you will either administer it or receive it.

Teaching and disciplining a child is a personal and individual practice: individual for the parent because most adults parent the way they were parented, individual for the child because what works with one may not work with another.

Discipline is used to teach right behavior. How it is <u>ministered</u> will differ from one parent to another and what is <u>effective</u> will differ from one child to another.

One child may be a pleaser. One disappointing look from you causes remorse and change. Another child may need a good, thorough explanation for why he's not to do something and that alone will keep him from doing it again. Yet another child, in the same family, may be very strong-willed and couldn't care less about your disappointing looks or listening to the reasons why a certain behavior is unacceptable—he's determined he will do what he wants to whether you like it or not. This child may not get the message that he needs to alter his behavior to fit your desires until he receives more firm discipline such as a spanking (not to be confused with a beating), time-out, grounding, or the suspension of privileges.

Depending upon your relationship with that child, different methods will be used. When I was growing up, all it took from my dad was a look of disappointment and I would start to cry and be so sorry. I would "never do it again." My mom, on the other hand, had to take sterner action with me. Our relationship was different from what I shared with Dad. I was with Mom more, therefore I was more familiar with her. Consequently she had to do more than just look at me to teach me right behavior—she had to take action. Did I love my dad more than my mom? No, we just had a different relationship.

Train up a Child

Discipline is not an option and neither is proper training. Proverbs 29:15 says, "The rod of correction imparts wisdom, but a child left to himself disgraces his mother." A sure way to be disgraced by your own child is by not taking the time to instruct and discipline him. What does a "child being left to himself really mean"? In Hebrew the word "left" is shalach, meaning to send away, to let depart, be pushed away or forsaken. Forsaken means to abandon or desert. Discipline and teaching takes both time and energy. If we are not actively involved in this, we are forsaking our child.

Most every child will test the limit at some time. They are watching to see if the adults in their life care enough about them to enforce the rules. Don't disappoint them.

Teaching and discipline are essential to the developmental process of a child. Your rules and expectations are like the guardrails on a narrow bridge. With the guardrails in place, you feel comfortable crossing over a bridge that is high in the sky. You know the rails will keep you from plummeting to the ground. They are there to protect you and keep you from falling. The same is true of your rules; they are in place to help your children cross their bridges and keep them from falling.

Unfortunately, we have a society full of children who are fatherless—who are either physically absent or emotionally uninvolved, thus leaving the disciplining to mom. If she is too stressed out and overburdened herself, the children will be left to raise themselves. They are not equipped for the job.

God intended for parents to nurture, train, and discipline their children. Investing time in raising our children is still valuable in the sight of God although society tries to diminish its importance. If a child does not have an authority figure interested in him—one who cares enough about him to call him into account when he makes bad choices—he could become fearful and angry.

Appropriate boundaries must be set and enforced. Make them age-appropriate. The more responsible the child, the more privileges he should enjoy. Our teenagers always had a curfew. They enjoyed the privilege of going out but they also had the responsibility to make it home on time. If they didn't get home on time, an appropriate discipline was given, such as, if they were half an hour late, the next time they wanted to go out, they had to come home a half an hour earlier than their normal curfew time.

The Value of Time

Our society is so busy with "stuff" that it's hard to carve out time to be with the family. It used to be that most every family had dinner and usually breakfast together. In today's society, very few families have dinner together on a regular basis. So much is lost from not sharing this one meal a day together. There's something to be said about sitting around the table and eating together, inviting conversation, which in turn leads to teaching children naturally. If you are not enjoying just one meal a day together as a family, try to fit it into your schedule. Make it a priority and see how your relationships will benefit from it.

Our culture perpetuates the lie that quality time is better than quantity. When we have quantity time, quality time just happens. Those teachable, happy moments that you couldn't have planned have an opportunity to happen if you spend time together on a regular basis—and I'm not talking about sitting in front of the television together. I have learned from reliable sources that the average father spends about 30 seconds a day engaging his children in one-on-one conversation. This is a tragedy! It takes time to know a child, time to impart truth to him, time to listen to and understand him and it also takes time to teach and discipline him. "Quality time" alone doesn't allow for that.

The greatest gift we can give our children is our time. A huge home is not what they need, a fancy car to ride in is not what they need, and the most expensive clothes are not what they need. They need us. A child feels valued and loved when a parent considers raising him to be more important than any other job that he or she has. Much of what we teach our children is caught, not taught: caught through spending time together, caught by the child watching you as you respond in certain situations, caught by watching you live out your values, and caught by seeing that you do what you tell him to do; this takes both quantity and quality time with your child.

Many times it's actually easier to leave a child to himself, especially if he has a bad attitude. Let's face it: children are a lot of work! But once you've made the commitment to be a parent or stepparent, you are accountable to God as to how you teach your child. It's pretty hard to teach and discipline your child if you aren't spending time together.

Discipline Requires Relationship

In a blended family situation, the rules for the parents are different. The stepparent should come alongside the natural parent and support their rules and how they enforce them. The natural parent already has expectations and runs the household and children in a certain way. The stepparent cannot come in and change everything or he will set himself up for a lot of resentment and rebellion. If both adults bring children into the marriage, agree on the rules and share them with the kids together.

It is usually best for the natural parent to administer the discipline. The child receives discipline better from his own parent, which leaves less room for him to resent his stepparent. This also keeps the stepparent from becoming the "bad guy." Both adults are equal in their authority in the home over the children, but the stepparent should come alongside the natural parent and support her in her decisions concerning the child.

Try to portray a united front before the children at all times. Of course, you are not going to agree on everything, but if you can discuss your differences, come to an agreement, and then present your decision to your child through the natural parent, then disciplining will be received better and training will have taken place.

If the child thinks you are not in agreement, he can manipulate the situation and before you know it, you and your spouse are arguing, and the discipline of the child, which was the goal, is overlooked or becomes harsher than it should have been.

Until the stepparent has had an opportunity to develop a bond with the child, discipline is better left to the natural parent. Bonding will take differing amounts of time depending on the individuals involved. Some adults naturally and easily relate to children, but others have a difficult time relating even to their own children. Some children are open and some are not, some are accepting of new people, some are not.

It's been said that the stepparent should wait a year to discipline a stepchild but I believe it depends on the relationship they've established. Some will build a relationship quickly in which the child and adult are interested in pursuing a close friendship from the start, while another relationship could take years to build for whatever reason.

The stepchild must know that his stepparent loves him, cares about him, and has his best interests at heart before the stepparent administers discipline. As Josh McDowell, author and speaker, says, "Rules without a relationship equal rebellion." A stepparent can actually cause a child to rebel if he imposes harsh rules and demands on the child when he hasn't taken the time to get to know the child.

The disciplining of the children in a "normal" family can be an area of division and strife, but in a blended family the problems can be multiplied. Favoritism, jealousies, harshness, treating a child differently because he's not yours, and siding with your own child over the stepchild are issues that most normal families don't have to deal with compared with a blended family.

That is why the adults should develop certain house rules that everyone must follow. Write them down if necessary. Fewer rules are better, so pick a few important ones. State what they are in a positive attitude so the children will not feel threatened by them.

With older children, drawing up a contract could be helpful. Make sure they know what the rules are and what is expected of them. Don't make so many harsh rules that the children get discouraged. The goal is to help and teach them to become responsible adults.

Clean Up Your Mess!

When Vicki moved into her father and stepmom's house at the age of 16, she came with some habits that just didn't work in her new home. She continually left empty, dirty glasses and plates all over the house. She didn't clean up after herself, which caused problems for the whole family since the younger children had been taught to clean up after themselves and they had been trained to eat at the kitchen table. Vicki's bedroom was a disaster as well. She had so many dirty bath towels in the room that the rest of the family didn't have any clean ones to use.

She was asked over and over by her parents to please be an example to her younger siblings by cleaning up her own mess and eating at the table like everyone else. But she just wouldn't do it. After several attempts at talking and reasoning with her, Vicky's parents knew they needed to take some real action.

They devised a plan together and laid it out for Vicky. From that point forward she was required to eat only at the table and clean up her own mess. This rule included snacks. If she chose to eat somewhere else in the house and leave a mess, she would pay the consequences.

First, she would be required to clean up all the dishes anyone used all day long. If that didn't work, she would not be allowed to enjoy any extra snacks from the pantry. She could only eat at home when the family sat down at mealtime (obviously, she ate lunch at school). They had to be stern with Vicky for a time; she did clean up everyone else's dishes a few times and she went a while without the privilege of having snacks between meals, but she finally learned and did what her parents asked.

As far as the towels were concerned, she was required to put them in the laundry so they could be washed and used by everyone. Her parents decided to simply close the door to her room rather than make that an issue as well. They chose their battle wisely—the one that was affecting others around her.

Agree on a Plan

Ongoing communication between marital partners should be a priority. Things that come up should be dealt with in a reasonable amount of time so that the problem doesn't become bigger than it really is.

If at all possible, let the natural parent do the disciplining while the stepparent builds a relationship. If the natural parent cannot do the disciplining, the child should be made aware that the stepparent is acting on behalf of the natural parent. Before the natural parent leaves the house, the children must know that the spouse has authority to enforce the rules on the natural parent's behalf (not unlike a babysitter).

Pray together as a couple but also pray as a family. A popular and true saying is "A family that prays together stays together." Ask God for wisdom in raising, teaching and disciplining the children. Ask for unity in your marriage so that together you can raise your children to become responsible, contributing and balanced adults.

If a child senses a crack in parental unity, he will use it to his own advantage. He will play on your emotions and manipulate the situation to gain power in his position. Be aware of this. The most important relationship to work on in any family is the marriage. If it is intact and working well, the rest of the relationships will profit from it.

Try to treat the children fairly, without favoritism. It is natural to favor your own child over anyone else's, even your spouse's child. But if you are aware of this and try to avoid doing it, your family will blend much easier. The children can tell if you are fair or if you're always siding with one child over another, which can cause jealousies, competition, bitterness and strife, not only between the siblings, but between you and the child and you and your spouse.

Try to spend individual time with each child, especially your stepchild, so you can get to know his heart, his fears, concerns, his dreams and hopes. Once you know someone's heart, it is much easier to love and accept them.

Eternal Consequences

Discipline in love. The way you discipline your children is setting the stage for how they will interpret God. Will they see Him as harsh and unforgiving? Will they think He is angry or uninvolved? Or will they believe He is a loving and caring Father? How they see you is how they will see their Heavenly Father.

Learning to obey parents has eternal value. The Lord commands "Children obey your parents in the Lord, for this is right. Honor your father and mother which is the first commandment with a promise that it may go well with you and that you may enjoy long life on the earth" (Ephesians 6:1–3). As your children learn to honor and obey you and their stepparent, they will be able to obey the Lord in His instructions to them. If they haven't learned to obey you, it will be harder for them to obey the Lord. Even if they resist your efforts, don't back down. In the long run, they will realize you loved them enough to hold them accountable and that alone could soften their heart to you and to the Lord.

We have all been around a "spoiled" child, one that is demanding and always wants his own way. That child has difficulty with relationships and obedience. No one wants to be around him for long. The spoiled child needs someone to take the time to train and discipline him so he will be liked by others and get along in the world.

In training your children, be consistent and fair. Don't show favoritism and make sure the discipline is fitting for the child and appropriate for the offense. Don't be guilty of forsaking your child.

Spotlight on Our Discipline

Instant Replay: Discipline is meant to teach right behavior, never to release my frustrations.

Self Examination: What image comes to mind when I think of the word discipline? If it is anything other than a tool meant to teach and train, I must renew my mind so I can discipline my children properly.

Action: Are my spouse and I in agreement as to the house rules and how to administer discipline when it is needed? If not, we will communicate and make a plan. If we need to invite a third party in as a mediator, we will.

Chapter 8

The Dangers of Resenting

"Love is patient, love is kind...it is not easily angered; it keeps no record of wrongs." 1 Corinthians 13: 4,5

Resentment can settle in on a family without its members even being aware that they've been trapped. This is a snare of the enemy that must be realized and dealt with, as it can especially be a problem in blended families.

To resent means, according to Webster, to feel or show displeasure and indignation at a person whom you feel has injured or offended you. Indignant means to be displeased. The word resent, broken down, is re and sent. The offense, wound, or irritation is re-sent to your thoughts and emotions causing you to feel the offense again and again thus making it hard to let it go. The enemy loves this type of thing because it keeps the offense alive and keeps the people apart.

Resentment may or may not be justified. You could have a legitimate reason for feeling displeasure with someone. That person may have hurt you, displayed un-thankfulness toward you and all that you've done for him, or he may continually choose to disregard you.

Guard Your Heart

Although we may be able to justify resenting someone, it is not helping you. In 1 Corinthians 13, which is known as the love chapter, God says in verse 5 that "Love is not rude, it is not self-seeking, it is not easily angered, <u>it keeps no record of wrongs.</u>"

Two reasons why resenting one another is more common in blended families are jealousy and a lack of bonding. Jealousy because of the relationship your spouse and his/her children enjoy with each other and the time that it takes away from you and vice versa, or jealousy because your spouse treats his/her own children with favoritism over yours and gives them more understanding and grace. The list could go on and on.

A lack of bonding is a major cause of resentment for all members. The stepchild was not born to you, you didn't care for him when he was an infant, you didn't change his diapers, see him take his first steps or hear him say his first words. You weren't there to catch him when he fell.

Stepsiblings were not born into a family together so they didn't experience the same home life, same traditions or same parents. Bonding just hasn't taken place. To bond means to glue or stick together through just about anything. It is the "glue" that holds everyone together regardless of who is doing what.

Because parents usually bond with their natural children, when the children get out of line or even act totally ugly, the parent disciplines them and at the end of the day, they hug them, forget the bad behavior and go on. Ill feelings do not set in because you love them and they love you. You accept them the way they are so it's easy to move ahead and start each day fresh. Sometimes parents even make excuses for their children's inappropriate behavior simply because they have bonded. This isn't so with the stepchildren because you have not bonded with them. You aren't glued or bound to them, so daily irritations that arise can become major battlefields.

Bonding is very important to the cohesion of a family. One way you as the adult can attempt to bond with your stepchild is to spend individual time with him or her. Get away from the house, just the two of you and go someplace where you have to interact with each other. Go somewhere that your stepchild would enjoy (maybe he/she could pick the place) and then ask God to help you to enjoy each another. Take time to talk and tell stories to your stepchild. If your relationship is very strained, maybe open the conversation up by reading a book on a particular subject that you'd like to discuss.

Try to have time alone with your stepchild on a regular basis so that bonding can occur. It won't happen the first time you do something alone; it takes time. This was so important to our relationship that the Lord required me to do something I really did not want to do. Home school our nephew. He wanted us to have lots of time alone together for the main purpose of bonding.

Nelson and I were home together every day, all day. He required so much attention and time that by the time my children got home from school, I had nothing left to give them. When my husband got home from work at 5:30, I was usually pulling my hair out and demanding him to take over with the strenuous challenge of caring for Nelson. As I look back at that time, it was one of the most difficult periods in our home life, but also one of the most valuable.

Nelson and I bonded in a way that couldn't have happened had we not had all that time together. Our children learned that obedience to God is more valuable than our own comforts and we all learned to open our hearts and home to one who needed a hand. Today, we are very close. We have had our share of problems but Nelson has a family who he knows loves him and is willing to sacrifice for him.

Today he is going to college as he wants to become an attorney. We joke that he owes us a portion of what he makes due to all the arguing he practiced on us! We enjoy being together. He calls my husband "Dad" and me "Mom" and we call him our "Son." The Lord used that time of sacrifice to develop our character and to teach us how to give. We each had our times of resentment though— Nelson wishing he could be with his birth mom, me resenting all the time and energy required by Nelson, Ron having to deal with a wife who couldn't deal with this kid anymore, and our own children resenting having to share their parents. The Lord was faithful, though and brought us through. Our children consider Nelson to be their brother. To think of him as a cousin or a nephew now is foreign. Nelson says we are his family. He sees his birth mom and half-brothers but feels a part of us too, which he is.

Victory and Freedom

Resentment ran rampant in Eric and Sue's home for years. They were a couple in which both of them had been married previously; Sue did not have children with her first husband but Eric had two with his first wife, a boy and a girl. After two years of marriage, they began trying to have a child of their own. It took five years of trying before they received the happy news that Sue was with child. They rejoiced, planned, and looked forward to the arrival of their little bundle of joy. They had been every-other-weekend parents to Eric's children but now they would have one of their own. They bonded to Ashley, their long awaited daughter, long before she was born. Finally she arrived and so did Cherise, Eric's 12 year old daughter, who came to live full-time with her dad and step mom.

The honeymoon period with Cherise lasted about three months. Sue had waited to have a baby for so long that anything or anyone who would interfere with her giving full attention to her child became reason for resentment. Sue had a difficult postpartum, and having to deal with a pre-teen along with her newborn was too much. She wanted to deal with the newborn but not with the 12 year old. She had looked so forward to having Ashley but having a 12-year-old move in at the same time was not what she had anticipated, expected, or wanted. Resentments began to build as Cherise required attention and time that was meant for Ashley.

Cherise had her own set of resentments—for one, having to obey a woman who was not her mother. Fights were the norm as tension, accusation, and irritation mounted. Cherise had an appropriate amount of chores to do but these became major problems in the home due to the ill feelings that had begun to erode their relationship. Eric became a referee, usually siding with Sue and maintaining her position as the mom of the home and insisting that she be respected. Cherise complained continually to her dad that she "had to do excessive amounts of work around the house and all that Sue did was play with the baby." Eric had had enough and so, wanting to prove to Cherise that Sue did much more than she realized, Cherise was required to interview and write a report on each family member's household duties. She was so amazed at how much her step mom really did that she never again complained that Sue didn't do enough around the house.

After six very long resentment-filled years, Cherise moved out to attend college. Sue resented Cherise for taking time and energy away from her own daughter, Cherise resented having to obey this woman who was not her mom, and Eric resented the fact that they couldn't get along! As soon as Cherise left, Sue "gutted" her room. She wanted to make sure Cherise would not be returning.

There was very little contact between Cherise and her parents during that first year of her moving out. Then something happened. Sue's mom passed away and she says she couldn't have made it without her siblings. God used this to speak to Sue about Ashley's need to have Cherise in her life. She loved her daughter more than she resented Cherise so she began to call her and invite her over for Ashley's sake.

Well, God had restoration in mind for Sue and her stepdaughter. Both of their attitudes totally changed toward each other. They began to enjoy each other's company and they came to the place where they could talk openly about the past. They forgave each other of real or imagined hurts. Sue says it's difficult to remember how very hard it was back then because they enjoy each other so much now.

Cherise recently had a daughter of her own. Sue couldn't be more proud of her grandbaby. Cherise has asked Sue to come and stay with her and the baby (she and her husband live five hours from Eric and Sue) and Sue has been delighted to do so. Their relationship is a healthy mother/daughter/friend relationship. Cherise realizes now, after having a child of her own, the awesome gift God gave her as a teen, in her dad and stepmom. They gave her stability, rules, and consistency and as Cherise puts it "I was safe in their home."

Cherise and Ashley have a normal, healthy and fun sister relationship. Though they are 12 years apart, they like having time together. Sue is certain that they will be there for each other should something happen to one of their parents. This kind of restoration and redemption was made possible through prayer.

The family couldn't get past resenting one another while Cherise was in the home but God used the death of Sue's mother to reunite this mother and stepdaughter and thus the whole family. God is in the business of bringing about something good from something bad. If they could have let go of resentment earlier, their home life would have been a happier place for everyone.

Resentment is a **choice**: you can choose to hang onto it or you can choose to let it go. You and your family will be better off if you all choose to let it go. It doesn't matter if the children are at home or not—start where you are now and build a relationship that is free of resentment.

Choose Love

Resentment leads to anger and if this is not dealt with appropriately, it will lead to bitterness. Bitterness is like cancer. Don't let it take root or it will overtake you.

One way to determine if resentment is clouding your relationship is to ask yourself if you have ever caught yourself dealing with your stepchild more severely or harshly than you would handle your own child. Do you play back in your mind the things they have "done to you?" Is it hard to forget their bad behavior and do you find yourself picking on them? Do little things annoy you about them, but if your child did them they wouldn't even be an issue?

Are you just hanging on doing your best to tolerate them so you can keep some peace in your home, or do you ignore them, trying to pretend they aren't even there? I applaud you for trying so hard but the Lord has an easier way. He says in Matthew 11: 28-30 "Come to me, all you who are weary and burdened, and I will give you rest. Take my yoke upon you and learn from me, for I am gentle and humble in heart, and you will find rest for your souls. For my yoke is easy and my burden is light."

Resentment is an underlying feeling of displeasure with someone such that, no matter what they do, you will be displeased. If you allow resentment to continue, they will stop trying to please you in any way. They will lose hope of pleasing you and will eventually give up trying.

You may be feeling resentment toward your spouse because he does not act any more grown up than the children do. He is making choices that just rub you the wrong way. Resenting someone will never cause him or her to change.

Resenting is a matter of the heart. Examine yourself. Are you resenting anyone? Whether you feel justified or not, you must let it go. It's a choice and you will benefit by releasing it.

No matter how much we try to hide our resentment, it will come out somehow. The person we resent will know it and it could cause much anguish, particularly if that person wants to please us.

Jesus says in Luke 17: 1, 2 (King James Version) "It would be better for him that a millstone were hanged about his neck, and be cast into the sea, than that he should offend one of these little ones." Offend here means to cause a child to sin, which could be a result of displaying anger, resentment, or displeasure toward him on a regular basis. We can resent our child to the point of exasperating him. We shouldn't be a cause for his justified anger. Remember, "Rules without a relationship equal rebellion." Though it's hard and you may not like your stepchild much, it will be worth your time to get to know him. Feelings oftentimes follow actions. I can guarantee that if you are determined to get to know your stepchild and develop an attitude of liking him, you will be rewarded in the long run.

Ephesians 6:4 says "And, ye fathers, provoke not your children to wrath; but bring them up in the nurture and admonition of the Lord." Children are not stupid. They sense whether someone likes them and is accepting of them but they can also sense if someone dislikes them, resents them, or wishes they weren't around. In a blended family, when you married your spouse, you got a package deal. You can't have your mate without receiving his children.

Resentment, love, anger, bitterness and acceptance—these are all choices. I can choose to love someone or resent him. I can choose to control a relationship through anger or I can choose a better way. The choice is mine. Once I decide to choose God's way, He will help me if I ask Him. Resentment is not of the Lord. If it's not of the Lord, then it is of the enemy.

Get Free!

How can we get rid of resentment if we have it toward someone? The first step is to acknowledge it. Examine yourself honestly.

Second, confess your resentment (sin) to yourself and to God. Ask God to forgive you and maybe even the person you have resented.

Third, repent! Agree that it is wrong and that you do not want to be a part of it any longer. Decide and choose in your heart not to allow it anymore.

Fourth, ask God to change your heart toward the person you resent. Ask Him to pour His love into your heart toward him or her.

And finally, do something really nice for him. He will feel good and so will you. This could be the thing needed for a new beginning in your relationship.

The enemy does not want you free so he will try to bring back to your mind the reasons you resent that person in first place. Don't go there. Guard your heart and mind.

Spotlight On My Heart

Instant Replay: Resent means to feel or show displeasure with a person. It is resending his or her offense back to my thoughts and emotions over and over again. The one I continually resent knows it.

Self Examination: Who do I resent? Even if I feel justified, it is wrong and it is not doing them, our relationship, or me any good. If I am resenting my stepchild, it is hurting my marriage relationship as well.

Action: I will release resentment by following the steps listed above. If I am not ready to let it go, I will ask God to help make me willing to let it become a thing of the past.

Chapter 9

Feel Like Giving Up?

"Find rest, O my soul, in God alone; my hope comes from Him.   He alone is my rock and my salvation; he is my fortress, I will not be shaken."   Psalm 62: 5,6

Ruth's heart was just not ready for the untimely death of her young husband.   You too may have lost someone through divorce or death who meant the world to you. You thought you had a future together but it was snatched away. Ruth wasn't sure how she would carry on now that her husband was gone. She didn't want to return home to her family because she had married outside of their beliefs. But at last she found the courage she needed to move ahead through her mother-in-law and the God she served.

Have you ever wished someone would give you back what has been taken from you? Maybe you've lost precious years in relationships because of strife and disunity or maybe you have lost your good health or material possessions. I've got good news

88

for you. There is someone to whom you can turn to recover these valuable things. His name is "Redeemer."

Looking for Help

Remember the Book of Job? Job lost everything, including all ten of his children, his health and his wealth. He was so pitiful that his wife told him to curse God and die. But he wouldn't give up. He called on God who was his redeemer and God recovered all these things for him, and more. Everything was restored to him even though his so-called comforters fervently accused him that the loss he was experiencing was his own fault. They told him he must have done something terribly wrong to deserve this.

Even in the midst of his incredible loss, pain, and accusation he looked to God, his Redeemer, because no one else could help or comfort him. He couldn't even help himself. He was afflicted with painful sores from the top of his head to the soles of his feet. All he could do was sit and scrape his body. But there is One greater than the worst circumstance.

In the first chapter of the Book of Ruth, Naomi, her husband Elimelech and their two sons, had gone to live in Moab due to a famine in Israel. They were from Bethlehem; their intention was to return to Israel when the famine was over. They went there to survive the famine, but the lives of all three males were required of them in this foreign land. Both of Naomi's sons had married Moabite women who were gentiles, which meant they served gods other than the true God of Israel. One son's wife was called Orpah and the other was Ruth. Naomi and her two daughter-in-laws had all become widows.

Naomi heard that the famine in Israel had come to an end so she prepared to return home, a childless widow. She was ready to return alone and empty-handed but Ruth determined to go with her even though Naomi had released her to return to her family and their gods. Ruth chose Naomi and the true God over her own family and their idols. She chose the unknown over the familiar. As far as we know, she'd never been away from Moab, her family and their security, but she was willing to become a foreigner without the protection of a husband.

She insisted on going with Naomi back to Bethlehem and told her, "Don't urge me to leave you or turn back from you, where you go I will go and where you stay I will stay. Your people will be my people and your God my God." (Ruth 1:16). She had heard stories about their God and how He delivered them out of Egypt, how He cared for them in the desert and had brought them victory in conquering the Promised Land. She realized there was something very different about their God in comparison to the deaf and dumb idols she had been taught to worship.

This was the key to Ruth's success. She chose God, the Redeemer, and His ways, thus allowing Him to give her back all and more of what she had lost.

Though Ruth had never been to Bethlehem in Judah, she was faithful to stay with her mother-in-law and vowed that nothing would separate them but death. Naomi could not promise her anything, but Ruth was determined to remain with her anyway. Naomi's daughter-in-law, Orpah, who had been married to her other son, had understandably chosen to go home to her own family after the death of her husband. She is never mentioned again in Scripture. However, Ruth has a whole book written about her. She was willing to give up all for a woman who had lost everything. The only thing she had left was her God. But He was enough!

Once in Bethlehem, Ruth continued to serve Naomi by gleaning in the fields any grain left by the harvesters so they could have something to eat. This could have been a very dangerous task, especially for a single woman.

Naomi pointed Ruth to the fields of Boaz who was a relative on her husband's side. He saw her gleaning in his field one day and inquired about her. He liked what he heard and immediately became her provider and protector. He told his foreman not to let any of the men touch her and she was invited to drink from his water jars when she was thirsty. He then told the harvesters to pull out some stalks for her to pick up. She no longer got the leftovers. Boaz then asked her to come and eat at his table, so she ate until she was full and there was plenty left over for her to take back to Naomi.

Later, Ruth went to Boaz at night at the instruction of Naomi, who was hoping he would become their redeemer. After he lay down at the far end of the grain pile he had just winnowed, she approached him quietly, uncovered his feet and lay down. This was traditionally a request for marriage. When Boaz awakened suddenly and realized someone was at his feet, he asked, "Who are you?" When she answered that it was Ruth, he blessed her and was pleased to hopefully take her as his wife.

However, there was a kinsman-redeemer (a male relative who restores or gets back for you what you have lost) closer to the family than Boaz who had first rights to buy Elimelech's (Naomi's husband) property and thus receive Ruth as his wife. Boaz hoped he wouldn't do it. And he didn't. The man didn't want to risk his own estate so he said he was unable to buy the land or take Ruth to be his wife.

So Ruth married Boaz, who loved her and took care of all of her needs as well as Naomi's. It was said of Boaz regarding Naomi that "He will renew your life and sustain you in your old age." (Ruth 4:15a). So Boaz, their kinsman-redeemer, gave back to them all that they had lost and he was very good to them.

This is a picture of what God wants to do for you. He wants to redeem all that has been taken away from you. What does He require of you? Just like Ruth, He asks only that you choose Him and let Him be your Savior and friend.

No one else cares about your pain, loss, and hopelessness like He does. Boaz was merely a man but he protected, provided for, cared for, loved, and was good to Ruth simply because she chose him. How much more will God, your Creator, do those same things for you? Don't give up hope; it is your lifeline.

Redeemed!

You might say these are just Bible stories and that God doesn't really give you back what this evil world takes from you. I can speak from personal experience that He still redeems today.

Within a three-week period, I separated from my first husband, and lost my home and job! Then, after moving back home with my parents, my father died unexpectedly at the age of 52. My dad was my anchor; he was going to help me get back on my feet. I felt stripped naked, like everything important to me had been taken. I clung to the Lord because He was my only hope and the only One who could return to me what I'd lost.

It took time, but He healed my broken heart and blessed me with a new and wonderful husband. We own a beautiful home and I have a purpose now, not just a job.

During that devastating time, I became intimate with God and came to know Him as my Father. He redeemed my situation because I turned to Him and He gave me back more than what I had before.

Even though your marriage might be hanging on by a thread, your children may be rebellious, your so-called blended family may not be blending at all, and you're not quite sure you can make it through another day, look to your Redeemer. What did he do for Job? Job and his wife birthed 10 more children, his health was restored all of their wealth, and more was returned to them, and his reputation was reestablished. I hope your situation isn't as bad as Job's was, but even if it is, your Redeemer lives. Put your hope in Him, not in your circumstances. Don't believe the lie that it will never get better. Believe in your Redeemer and speak new life into your situation.

It doesn't matter where you come from, where you've been, what sins you've committed, or what idols you've worshipped. What matters now is that you choose God and His ways. He can take any horrific situation and turn it around and make good come out of it (Romans 8:28). That is what He wants to do for you. He can cause your blended family to flourish even though you are not blood-related. You are related through Christ and that can become a stronger bond than a blood tie.

Let Him Fix It

David wrote the Psalm at the top of this chapter when he was being hunted down like a criminal when he had done nothing wrong. But he put his hope in God; he knew no one else could help him. That is all I am encouraging you to do.

Determine to fix your eyes on God and not your circumstances. He will come through for you. He really is the answer to life's most difficult problems. He does not have favorites. What He did for Ruth, Job, David and me, He will do for you.

Spotlight On My Situation

Instant Replay: My Creator cares about my family, our situation, and me. He is able and willing to redeem all that I (we) have lost.

Self Examination: Have I truly committed my situation to the Redeemer? Do I have peace, trust and hope that He will come through?

Action: Since God can work miracles and I can't, I will put my hope and trust in Him. I will be obedient to do what He tells me. I trust He will help our family to blend and will help us in any other area where we need a Redeemer. I choose to speak life into my family and our circumstances.

Chapter 10

Loving the Unlovable

"Be imitators of God, therefore, as dearly loved children and live a life of love, just as Christ loved us and gave himself up for us as a fragrant offering and sacrifice to God."
Ephesians 5:1, 2

Ever been around someone who bugged you so much that you couldn't stand being in the same room with him? Or have you met someone who is so off the wall that he seems to have come from another planet? Everything he does and says rubs you the wrong way. Or maybe he has an annoying habit that if he does it just one more time in your presence you're going to scream (or do something worse)! We've all had someone like this in our lives but have we handled it well?

Mary learned to handle it well. She's to the place now where she can say she really does love the girl who used to be her daily source of irritation and frustration. Sherry was not anything like the daughter Mary hoped she was getting when she married the young girl's dad.

Suck It Up and Do It!

Tim and Mary were married within one year of them giving their hearts and lives over to the Lord. They had both been held captive to bondages that were destroying their lives, but when they met the Lord they each had a dramatic life-changing experience.

Mary's parents were very loving, caring, and involved. She was disciplined appropriately during her growing up years and knew her parents were there for her. She had a pretty "normal" childhood but when she entered high school she got in with the wrong crowd. She was rebellious and in spite of her parent's efforts to help her, the ultimate shock happened when, at the age of 16, she became pregnant. This was back in the day when if you got pregnant outside of marriage you didn't let anyone know about it. Her parents were extremely upset over this but were determined to stand by their daughter. They left it up to her whether she would keep the baby or give it up for adoption. Abortion was not an option that any of them considered.

She cried and begged her parents to tell her what to do but they felt she had to live with the decision and so she must make it herself. She finally, in the 8th month of pregnancy, felt she should give her baby up for adoption, which she did. She gave birth to a son and Mary gave the gift of this precious little bundle to another family to love and to raise.

Against her parent's wishes, Mary continued to see the baby's father. A few years later at the age of 21, she had another baby boy by him. This time, however, she kept her son whom she named Chad. She and the father of their babies never married and he never had much to do with the son she raised. She made a stable life for herself and her little boy, she worked hard and they were both reasonably happy. Then she met Sid. He inched his way into her heart and then her home. As Chad says, "When he moved in, he didn't come alone." He brought drugs, alcohol, confusion and strife. He didn't work much except to deal dope out of their home. Mary eventually quit her job because the drug scene was taking over her life too. Chad was very unhappy with Sid in their home and all the junk he brought with him, so Mary would tell her little boy they were going to leave Sid. She had meant it but after eight years they were still together.

During that time, she had several abortions and her life went from bad to worse. At the age of 34, she got pregnant again but this time, for some reason, she did not abort. She says God preserved her child through the pregnancy and her baby came forth healthy, even though she continued doing drugs during all nine months. She and Sid stayed together until their child was two years old. Then Mary became deathly ill and was placed in the hospital for quite some time.

Her mother Beatrice came to her aide. She cared for Mary's sons while she was so sick, but she also "cleaned house." She knew something was wrong in her daughter's life and finally the truth was exposed: Mary was a drug addict. Beatrice took charge and told Sid to get out of her daughter's home, which he did. She stayed with Mary many months after she came home from the hospital and helped her get clean of drugs.

When she was finally well enough, Mary went to church where she had a life changing encounter with the Lord. She totally gave herself to Him and He gave her a new life, a life worth living. She was radically delivered from all the things that had her bound. She began dating Tim, whom she had known during her drug days; he too had been a "druggy." But, he had met the same God and was totally transformed as well. They fell in love and felt it was their Lord's will for them to marry and so they did.

Mary had two boys, both by different fathers and Tim had a daughter, Sherry, from his first marriage. Sherry was 11 and the only girl in her daddy's life until Mary came along. She didn't like Mary and was determined that her dad would not remain with her. She had been molested when she was nine years old, and so she carried a lot of emotional baggage. She was a needy child who wanted her dad to herself.

Sherry and Chad got along great as siblings and they were good friends from the start. Sherry didn't like her new three-year-old little brother, however, and was extremely mean to him. She also disliked her new stepmom so much that she constantly tried to separate her parents in any way her young mind could think. The irony of it all was that when her dad wasn't home she would follow Mary everywhere and as she followed, she talked, continuously. She talked about anything and everything. She needed validation and strove to get it through talking which she aimed at Mary.

Mary said she occasionally said "Uh-huh" or "Oh, really?" just so Sherry knew she was hearing, but that was usually all that Mary got in.

Day after day, Sherry talked to Mary. She didn't like Mary but oh, how she needed her. Mary says that she knew she would never win her stepdaughter over through discipline; it would have to be through love. But Mary didn't love Sherry. She didn't like her either, and didn't appreciate her interference in her marriage and the way she would try to come between her and her husband. She also resented the way Sherry treated her three-year-old little boy. Mom and stepdaughter didn't find much in common nor did they find much to like about each other, but they were always together and Sherry was always talking.

Mary, as the adult in the relationship, knew she had to do something. She couldn't allow their ill feelings and bad attitudes toward each other to continue because one bad relationship in a family affects everyone. Mary began crying out to God to **give her His love** for His daughter, Sherry. She cried out over and over again and nothing seemed to change. Sherry continued to follow her around talking incessantly about nothing and driving Mary absolutely crazy. Mary allowed her stepdaughter to talk and talk and talk because intuitively, she knew this would be a key in winning favor with her. Mary didn't actually listen to all that Sherry had to say, but she would acknowledge her occasionally to make her think she was listening.

Mary also knew that, as the adult, how she treated and responded to her new daughter would determine, to a great extent, how their future relationship would be. Mary determined that, with God's help, she would love her daughter, accept her and leave the disciplining up to her husband. She often times felt like screaming at her to "shut up" and leave her alone, but through God's grace and help, she didn't.

Mary was learning what it means to walk after the Spirit of God and not after the flesh (Romans 8:1, paraphrased, King James Version). Walking after the Spirit means depending on the Spirit to help you, lead you, enable you, encourage you (so that you do not give up) and leaning on Him to help you live the way He wants. It is submitting yourself to Him, confessing you cannot do this thing by yourself, but realizing through Him all things are possible and that, together, you can do it. It is choosing to live your life to please God rather than yourself.

Living after the flesh is depending on yourself and gratifying your own desires like screaming at a child to shut up because she is bothering you. It is allowing the sinful nature that is innate in us to rule our lives. We can't "will" ourselves to love and treat another person the way we should, especially if the person is in our face and bugging us all day long! It just won't happen in and of yourself. You can give it a noble try, but true and lasting success and change will come only through the Spirit enabling you and changing you from the inside out as you depend on Him to transform you. He can change us so radically that we will be amazed at the love we have for the person who has been the nightmare of our lives. It may take some time but as you live by the Spirit and die to gratifying the flesh, you will overcome in the end.

A term my husband and I have used is **"prayority." Prayer must be a priority** in a family regardless if it is blended or not.

As the adults and parents of the family you have a responsibility to model reliance upon the Lord in every area of your life. One way is through prayer. Prayer says, "Lord, I need you and your help. I can't do this thing alone but I trust, with your help, I can." Even the humble position of kneeling reveals a dependence upon the Lord. I have never known God to fail a person who earnestly sought Him for His help. He is a very good Father and is waiting for us to invite Him into the situation.

When you're in the midst of what seems to be an impossible situation, take a moment to ask God for help and guidance. Then take a deep breath and believe Him to help you. Your situation may not change quickly but you are allowing God to work in you to change you and your attitude. If we are not growing as individuals and becoming more like the Lord, then we are actually backsliding. Isn't it true that if you're not going forward, you are standing still or going backward? We, as followers of Christ, should make it our goal to become more like Him and to "...be conformed into the image of his Son." (Romans 8: 29). That takes change on our part. Don't despise the situations and the people God allows in your life; realize they are the very tools He uses to make you more like His Beloved Son.

Mary's attitude toward her stepdaughter became one of grace. She realized, like Mary Magdalene in the Bible, that she had been forgiven much and shown incredible grace so, with God's help, she was emboldened to allow a child who didn't like her to follow her around and talk at her about gobble-de-goop. This would bug anyone, but especially when coming from a child who didn't want you there and who did what she could to get rid of you. But because Mary chose to submit herself to God and allow Him to love Sherry through her, her stepdaughter has arisen to call her blessed.

Why is that important? Why should we care about what our stepchildren think of us anyway? After all, we didn't marry them; we married their parent. Hopefully, one day soon, they will be gone and we won't have to deal with them anymore. But that is rarely the case—we will continue to deal with them even after they leave home. The reason it's important for you to get along with your stepchildren is because it will bring glory to God. It's that simple. Plus, your spouse will love you all the more for it. If we are followers of Christ, then we are to do what we can to live in peace and fellowship with all people especially those in our own family. When we make our blended families work, others will see and God will be glorified.

Your Rewards Shall be Great

Sherry wrote the following card to her stepmom testifying to the power of God to work in and through relationships when one party is willing to live by the Spirit and not the flesh. It took years, but because Mary didn't give up, she has received a part of her reward here on earth (the rest she will receive in Heaven) by enjoying a great relationship with her daughter. The message in the card is lengthy but is worth sharing in its entirety:

"Mom - You've Made a Difference in My Life

How do you tell the single most important woman in your life what a difference she's made—or how many times the sound of her voice has lifted your spirit and given you the courage to keep following the path of your dreams? How do you find the words to thank her for sacrifices she's made—for the ones you know about and the ones she's never told you of—and the countless times she put your needs above her own? Mom, I cannot put into words the way I feel about you, but I hope you always know in your heart how much I love you, respect you, and thank you for the countless ways you've helped make my life what it is today. Happy Mother's Day."

What Sherry wrote inside the card is just as good: "I love you, today, tomorrow and forever. Your Daughter, Sherry." And on the side page she wrote: "I can only hope that I am to my Baby what you are to me. You are the reason I am where I am today. I remember the day I cried because I didn't want you to have my name. Now I am proud to say that I have yours. When Dad married you he made the best choice he has ever made as far as I am concerned. With all my love."

This stepdaughter rose to call her mother blessed. Because Mary chose to live unselfishly and decided, with God's help, to love a child who drove her crazy, she is now reaping what she sowed. When Sherry was in labor with her baby, she insisted Mary be with her through the delivery. Mary is now a grandma and enjoying all that the role entails.

Determination

God loves all of His children whether we like them or not. He is not bugged by any of us, but understands and loves us (He does hate the sin we commit but it doesn't affect His love for each of us). 1 Thessalonians 4:9 says "...for you yourselves have been taught by God to love each other." When we submit ourselves to God, He can teach us to love someone who we don't even like! He can give us His heart and unconditional love for another person if we ask Him to do it and then submit ourselves to Him so He can love that person through us—thus causing us to love him or her.

As the adult, our response to our stepchildren will determine to a greater extent than theirs, how the relationship will eventually end up. We can choose to love them and speak life over them and our relationship with them, or we can choose to go around cursing and complaining about our stepchildren (or anyone for that matter). If we do the latter, then we are guilty of sowing further discontent and problems into their lives and our relationship with them. Love covers other people; it doesn't expose the things we dislike about them. If we choose to speak well of them (and sometimes this can only be done with God's help), eventually the things we speak will cause good things to come true, in them and in our relationship with them. This doesn't mean you deny the truth about them, but that you choose to speak life and goodness over them rather than negativity and death.

God can give us His love for someone we don't like or even want around us. It may take awhile because God also has to work in us, but if we are willing to let God do what He needs to do, we will eventually love even a child who truly bugs us! Be committed and don't give up—it will one day be worth it as we've seen with Mary and Sherry. See, it's not about us and our being comfortable. It's all about God and seeing His Kingdom established in our homes. It's all about raising Godly children who will love the Lord when they leave us, because they've seen Him modeled in our lives. Not that we have done everything perfectly, but that we had a heart to **want** to live our lives according to the Word of God.

The very thing that bugs you about someone (like continual talking) could be the key to winning him or her over. Because Mary was willing to let Sherry talk and talk and talk, Sherry finally came to the conclusion that Mary wasn't so bad after all. Sherry had a great need to be heard and Mary let her be heard. Mary didn't scream at her to shut up, even though she wanted to, but instead chose to submit herself to Christ to let Him love Sherry through her. When we submit to Christ, we are free to let Him do something through us rather than to try to make it happen ourselves.

The Bible says "As iron sharpens iron, so one man sharpens another." (Proverbs 27:17). God uses the people in our lives who we consider difficult to sharpen us, thus causing us to become the best we can be. If Sherry had not been in Mary's life, she may not have ever learned to love unconditionally. She may never have learned how to die to the flesh and live by the Spirit. These are invaluable rewards she has received.

By deciding to accept, as best she could with God's help, a little girl who thoroughly irritated her, she has become a better person. Her family is better too. She is the proud grandma of a baby girl. Had she not accepted Sherry, she probably would not be accepted now as a grandma to Sherry's child.

When we choose to live by the Book, we get to a higher place although it might be a rocky road getting there.

Spotlight On Love

Instant Replay: Life is about love.

Self Examination: Who do I need to start loving?

Action: I choose to start loving them today. I will live by the Spirit and not the flesh.

Chapter 11

Order In The Home

"Just as each of us has one body and many members, and these members do not all have the same function, so in Christ we who are many form one body, and each member belongs to all the others." Romans 12:4,5

As in any successfully working entity, there must be a leader who makes the final decision. Can you imagine a corporation where everyone just did what they wanted with no guidelines and no one to call the shots? It would be chaos with little valuable work being accomplished.

In a successful corporation, there is the "top" person at whose desk the "buck stops." He articulates the vision for the corporation and sees to it that the employees are working toward the company's goals. He is ultimately responsible for what takes place in the company of which he has been given charge.

The same is true in the home. There has to be one person who is ultimately responsible; otherwise there will be too many bosses and chaos would erupt. Even in the Trinity, God the

Father is the head over Jesus and the Holy Spirit (1 Corinthians 11:3).

Breaking the Cycle

James and Irene seem to be the perfect couple. They are both good-looking and talented. They are professionals and their income level allows them to spend freely. When they walk into a room, people notice.

James, however, is preoccupied with his profession. When he is home, he is in the office working. He doesn't take the time to talk with his wife so she feels lonely and unnoticed. When she brings this up to him, he feels attacked and unappreciated. James feels she should accept the fact that he works hard for the family and should quit expecting so much from him. Doesn't she know that he'll be done working when he's done? He can't be expected to "coddle" her after a hard day's work.

Due to the fact that James is withholding the love that Irene so desperately needs, she feels nothing but resentment and anger toward him. When he asks her to do something such as run an errand for him, she tells him to do it himself. They are slipping further and further apart. The more unloved Irene feels, the more disrespect she shows James. Even though it looks like they have it all, they are missing the essential ingredients that make for a happy, well-balanced marriage.

James is not taking the lead in his home by loving his wife, which just so happens to be her deepest need. She needs to feel adored and cherished by him but he has chosen to be too busy to meet this longing.

Since she feels so unloved, she fails to give him respect, which just so happens to be his greatest need. Men don't need love as much as they need respect. They have a deep yearning to be admired and revered.

James and Irene are in a cycle that many married couples unfortunately find themselves in. The way each couple gets into the cycle may be different, but they all find themselves going round and round. First, the wife feels unloved so she gives disrespect. He feels disrespected so he doesn't show her love. And it goes on and on. One of them needs to jump off of the merry-go-round and begin to offer to the other the love or respect that he or she is withholding.

In marriage, it's not about me! We entered a covenant to honor, love and cherish until death do us part. We didn't put conditions on it: "If they love me first, I'll love them back." Marriage is supposed to be a picture of Jesus and His bride. Jesus loves the church so much that He died for her and she in turn honors and respects Him.

If your marriage is not functioning properly, take a look at your role. You probably already know what your spouse is doing wrong but examine yourself. You cannot force another to step up to the plate and do what he or she should but you can choose to change yourself.

It's God's Design

God designed the family. Because of that, He has the right to say how it works best. There are certain things that each family member should do to ensure its success. Husbands are to love their wives, wives are to submit to their husbands and the children are to give their parents honor.

In Ephesians 5: 22,23 wives are mandated to submit to their own husbands as they do (or should do) to the Lord because the husband is the head of the wife. Wives, I can hear you now explaining that if your husband would only do the right stuff such as pray more and follow God then you could submit to him. But until you see him doing the things you think he should, you are not going to submit—not unless you happen to agree with him. This is the attitude of many wives today. We would submit if he would only get his act together. "Then he would be someone I could follow."

Ladies, I know what you're talking about, but I haven't found it in the Bible that we are to submit only if we think he's right. There are exceptions to this, of course. God doesn't ask you to submit if your husband is asking you to violate God's will or the law, and our Heavenly Father would never expect us to sit idly by while our husband abused our children or us. God is not hateful or mean and does not want us treated that way. If your husband is abusing you, he has forfeited his authority as head of the house, and you should do what you must to protect yourself and your children.

But in a family where the husband is not abusing anyone, even if you believe you can do a better job than he can of leading the family or of making decisions, you must learn to submit. Submission is not gritting your teeth and making yourself do what he says. It is really an attitude of giving him permission to lead.

You have the God-given right and the ability to express your opinions to your husband. You are both unique individuals, thus you will see things differently. You are neither a doormat nor are you to be overbearing. You are his helpmate; he needs your insight. If he is a wise husband, he will respect your counsel.

After you have discussed the issue together and have shared your opinions and you still disagree, you must submit to your husband and allow him to make the final decision without receiving wrath from you. Your attitude must be one of agreement. This is showing him the respect he needs. A husband cannot be in authority over his wife unless she allows him to be.

God's Design for Wives

God is not saying that women are not as smart as men or that they can't make as good a decision. He is saying that someone must ultimately be in charge and the Designer Of Families has chosen the man. This is an unpopular truth today, but one that should be followed. When two people live together they don't automatically agree on everything. One person has to be given the right to speak the final word so things will not remain at a standstill or move in different directions, resulting in the couple not moving ahead together. Without a leader, confusion sets in.

The husband is given the ultimate responsibility for what happens in the family. He must be accountable for what he did or did not do and for what was good in his family and what wasn't.

A wife must also be accountable, but if she submits to her husband and does not usurp his authority, he will actually serve as a covering for her. He will take the responsibility for the family. Women, if we can understand that the God-given authority our husbands have is to be a protection and covering for us, we should have an easier time accepting our different, but equally important roles.

It is built into your husband to be like an umbrella that shields you from the rain. Let him be that umbrella and accept the responsibility of protecting his family from the storms of life. God is not trying to take something away from you but instead He has given you a covering, a protector, and a defender. Encourage your husband by letting him know you appreciate his leadership.

Many wives struggle with trying to change their husbands. We want them made into what we think they should be. Many men live in quiet desperation not thinking anyone believes in them and not feeling respected, thus many of them quit trying to lead even their own families. We have lost this truth but we were made to be their helpmates, to come alongside them. For their good, as well as our own, we would be wise to build them up and give them the courage (through encouragement) to become all they were designed to be.

Obedience and submission are not the same thing. Obedience is something our children must do—they are to obey us and sometimes we have to make them do what we ask. But submission is a conscious decision to allow someone to have authority over you. Understand the difference? Obedience could be demanded but submission is given.

Though we could go into greater detail about the importance of submitting to our own husbands, we will end here by saying that the most important reason to submit is because that is what the word of God tells us. To receive God's blessing on our life, we must obey all of His Word, and not just the parts we like or agree with.

God's Design for Husbands

Ephesians 5:21 tells us to "Submit to one another out of reverence for Christ." Sometimes a husband will submit to his wife and allow her to make the decision simply because he loves her and wants to make her happy, or because he realizes she is right.

The ultimate responsibility of the husband is to "Love your wives as Christ loved the church and gave Himself up for her." What does this mean? You say, "Of course I love my wife, I married her didn't I?" But the Lord's love is unconditional. The description of His love is found in 1 Corinthians 13. Can you honestly say you love your wife this way, and will she agree with you? If you do, or are at least attempting to most of the time, your wife will feel special, cherished and loved. She will trust you if you love her unconditionally, thus she will be able to submit to you much easier. If she feels you have her best interests in mind, even if she disagrees with you, she will submit because she feels safe with you.

If you are more interested in what is best for you and "love" your wife with selfish motives, she knows it. But if she feels you are looking out for her and the children, she will want to follow you. Determine to start today to love your wife unconditionally and watch the transformation in her. I don't know of any wife who would not respond positively if she feels cherished. The things that used to come between you will melt away as she trusts your love and she will be willing to come alongside you as your helpmate.

God's Design for Children

The children, of course, are to honor all of the "parents" in their lives, "natural" or "step." They must never be allowed to speak disrespectfully to the parents, not even behind their backs. The parents must respect the children in their home. Respect their boundaries, privacy, and the simple fact that they are human; all people need respect. The child must be respected as an individual but he is actually commanded by God to honor his parents—he has no choice. To honor means to highly regard, to respect greatly and esteem. If you respect your children, they will find it much easier to honor you.

Siblings should be encouraged to treat each other as they would like to be treated. They should not be allowed to cross boundaries such as name-calling, aggression or snooping through another's room. They should never borrow something without permission from the owner. Meanness and bullying should not be tolerated because it only creates anger and resentment and will hinder or prevent the children from becoming friends.

Unity is Key

The sooner an atmosphere of unity is created in your home, the better you all will be. Unity is the quality of being one in spirit, purpose, and sentiment; it is harmony, agreement and uniformity. Have you ever met a family in which you knew the children were adopted but they looked and acted like the parents? It's amazing, but I believe it's because the children know they are loved, are in harmony with their parents and thus, somehow, they begin to take on their parents' looks and characteristics even though they were not born to them. They have become one family.

We've all seen a couple who seems to go together, not because they are both good-looking but because they have unity and a common respect for each other. This is obtainable for any of us if we are willing to apply Biblical principles to our daily lives, where it really counts.

Men: Love your wife! Women: Respect your husband! And both of you see to it that the children are honoring the two of you as you respect them.

It's normal to feel something special about your biological child that you simply don't feel toward your stepchild. God has given parents the capacity for deep love for their own children that is not naturally there for other people's children, but it can be obtained over time as you take on the responsibility to be a stepparent. Do all you can to nurture a relationship that is respectful, enjoyable, and comfortable for both of you. Demonstrate to your stepchild that you love him and are someone he can trust and therefore take pleasure in the relationship as it becomes fulfilling and special to both of you.

Spotlight on My Role

Instant Replay: God designed the family therefore He has the right to decide how it functions best. He gave roles to each member of the family unit.

Self Examination: How am I doing in my role? Am I doing my best in my God-given position?

Action: What am I going to do differently? Are my spouse and I on "The Cycle"? Make a decision to stop your part in it. How can I better love or respect my spouse?

Chapter 12

Q & A: Answers to Tough Questions

"But wisdom is proved right by her actions." Matthew
11:19b

**How can I develop a loving relationship with my adult
stepchildren who have homes and children of their own?**

Good question! My stepdad, Manny, did this exceptionally
well. He was married to mom for only 11 years but at his funeral,
all of us felt a great loss. He had won our hearts and affection by:

• Never interfering. When we first met him, we were not at all
sure about him. My dad had passed on and we wanted only the
best for mom. Manny did not push himself into our inner circle;
he stayed on the periphery, enjoying our stories and commenting
when referred to, but he never pushed his way in. Gradually, we
each invited him to be a part of our "family inner circle."

- He showed us that he accepted us just the way we were. He liked us and, when someone likes you, it's hard not to like them back.

- He never criticized us, though I'm sure he had reasons to.

- He never spoke badly about us; he always had a nice word to say.

- He acted like a Grandpa to our children. He spoiled them, gave them money, candy, and ice cream. He was just great fun for them to be around. He was the only grandpa our daughter Chelsea ever knew. He became part of us simply by accepting us.

My husband and I are expecting our first child together and we think it would be a good idea to have his daughter call me Mom. This might help her and me to bond. What is your opinion?

We asked my son, Keenan, to call my husband "Papa" soon after we were married. I recently asked him how he felt about it. He said he felt anger because he was not ready for it when we asked him to do it. Instead of helping the bonding process, it actually hindered it. We had expected Keenan to give a title to my husband that he was not ready to give.

Our nephew, on the other hand, after living with us for just a few short months asked us if he could call us Mom and Dad. Of course, we were delighted. The child should not be asked to do this—when and **if** they are ever ready, they will tell you. The biological parent can leave the door open suggesting that if the child would ever like to call his stepparent mom or dad that it would be quite all right.

Some children will never want to call their parent's spouse "Mom or Dad." They could have a wonderful, affectionate relationship with their stepparent but never feel the need or desire to call them anything but their name. Accept this without feeling like you have done something wrong. I never called my mom's husband "Dad," but I loved him and had a great relationship with him.

When one of the children stay at his other parent's home, is it okay to let his siblings play with his things as long as they respect his property?

No, children need to know that they have privacy and that their things will be untouched until they return. The child should be made to feel secure that his possessions are his and will not be used without permission. Children need their own space. Enforce this rule for all the children. You will build confidence that they and their things are respected in your home.

Should I compel the stepsiblings to play together so that they can become friends and thus promote bonding between them?

This is probably not a good idea. During family times, everyone should be encouraged to be a part of whatever the family is doing together. But in the day-to-day routine, let them have their own friends and play with whomever they want. Let the siblings develop their own relationship with just a few ground rules such as respect for one another, no name calling, no hitting and allowing one another the right to privacy.

Should I be concerned about sexual contact among older stepsiblings?

Yes! When I was growing up 40 years ago, I had a friend who was sexually involved with her stepbrother. Their parents, of course, never imagined that would happen right under their own roof!

Talk to your older kids about your expectations. Teach the girls and boys to dress modestly and not to walk around the house in front of their siblings in scanty clothing. Teach them to respect their sibling's privacy in their bedrooms as well as in the bathroom and that they should knock before entering. Have them close their bedroom doors while they dress; they may not have had to do this before the marriage.

Teach the kids that sex is a gift to a husband and wife but anything outside of a marriage contract is wrong. Be wise and don't leave them in vulnerable situations. Realize your teens, as well as your preteens, are curious about sex. Teach them about it and answer their questions. Don't act embarrassed and they won't be embarrassed to come to you.

The world is giving them the message that premarital sex and multiple partners are acceptable. You need to give them the truth. Be aware that siblings often want to experiment on each other. Educate them that this is wrong and why. Keep the lines of communication open so you can avoid or deal with any situation immediately that might come up.

We feel like we have done most everything wrong and our relationships prove it. What can we do?

Start where you are. Apologize to those you feel you have wronged. Try to make right any mistakes that you can. Many things can't be undone but you can start where you are and begin today to do what you know is right. Begin to love them unconditionally. It takes about ten positive comments to make up for a negative one so watch what you say and how you say it. It may take time for your family members to accept that you really are changing so don't get discouraged. Over time they will trust that you will not revert back to the same old patterns.

To help you change and keep you accountable, get together with some other blended families and form a support group for the purpose of encouraging and bouncing things off one another.

Ask each other how you're doing. This can be very beneficial; you can help them and they can help you.

James 5:16 talks about confessing your sins to each other so you can be healed. I have learned from experience that when you admit a problem or an area in which you want to change and bring it into the Light, you will be healed and changed. Hiding our sins only keeps us in bondage; we can't do any better if we are trying to pretend a problem doesn't exist. But when we admit we need to change in an area, the power to do so is released through our confession.

If you are obviously favoring your natural child over your stepchild, ask your stepchild to forgive you. Admit you have done this and tell her that you want to change. Then take her on a date and start showing her some favor. Let her begin to feel unconditional love from you.

Believe me, we made a lot of mistakes but our hearts were right in that we wanted our family to work. If you are willing to confess you have done some things wrong, admit what they are, apologize for them and then move in the right direction—your family will improve and so will your relationships.

My stepchild knows just what to do to get on my nerves. It seems like he tries to get me upset. How can I make him stop?

Don't give him what he wants, which is to get you upset. Don't overreact. Instead, when he purposefully irritates you, take the fun out of it for him. Ignore him, make a joke of the situation and laugh or remove him from your presence. Don't let a child have so much power over you that he can get you upset at his own whim.

Get your spouse on your side. Determine whether the child is just trying to get your attention, whether he is emotionally wounded and his acting out is aimed at you, or if he is really trying to sabotage you. Once the motive is decided, you can better deal with the situation.

Let the child know there are consequences for his behavior. He is the one who will suffer the penalty if he deliberately tries to upset you.

Make sure you are not overly sensitive and reacting to him in a way that is inappropriate. The child might just have a weird sense of humor and you aren't used to it. Or it could be just childish immaturity. Do not punish a child for being a child. That is why your spouse's input is so important to determine what the child is up to, if anything. Deal with him as you would your natural child. A support group would be invaluable as the members could help you to come up with a strategy that best fits your stepchild. If you determine he is doing his best to bug you, then think of a plan to take the fun out of it for him.

Is it important to let the kids have their own room? We would like an office but that means the kids would have to share.

If at all possible, give the kids their own rooms, especially if they had their own room prior to the marriage. Don't let them feel misplaced and demoted (particularly the older kids) because you married. Give them a place in your home that they feel is their own and where they can have privacy to do what they want.

If it is not possible, it's not possible! But do what you can to give them space to spread out and have time to be alone when it's needed.

Our nephew moved in with us at the age of 10. We did not have an extra room so he moved into Keenan's room who was 14 at the time. They lived together in that small room for almost three years. It wasn't easy for them but they worked it out. Actually since Keenan was so much older, he was in "charge." He taught Nelson to keep the room picked up and they learned to give each other space.

Our son's mother tells him one thing yet does another. Just recently, she promised to take him for the whole weekend. He was devastated when she didn't show up. How can we help him? We feel so bad each time something like this happens.

If you have tried reasoning with his mother and that doesn't work, all you can do is let him express his anger and disappointment. Encourage him to talk so he doesn't stuff his feelings. You may need to coach him in how he feels because he may not know. You could say something like "My heart is so sad for you that your mother didn't come as she said. How do you feel?" Don't put words into his mouth but communicate that you understand his pain.

Avoid criticizing his mother. This will not help and actually could put him on the defense for her. Just let him know you understand that she hurt him. Do not attempt to make excuses for her. She needs to take responsibility for her actions.

Convey to your child that it is not his fault that she didn't keep her word. So often kids internalize that something must be wrong with them and that is why their parent is acting that way. Let him know that adults are responsible for their own behavior.

My son's dad continually badmouths my husband to him. He's always telling him that "he is no good, he is not your dad, and you don't have to do anything he tells you. If he tries to make you do something, tell me and I'll set him straight." This is causing big problems between my husband and son since my son has little regard for what my husband says.

This is a very difficult situation. Your ex-husband is very insecure about his place in his son's life. He is threatened by your husband's role in the life of your child; therefore, he is doing everything he can to keep them from developing a congenial relationship. This is unfortunate, particularly for your child who has not only had to endure the separation brought about by divorce, but who is now put in the middle to choose sides.

There are a few things you can do to try to help remedy this situation. First, you want your ex husband to be secure in his role as "Dad." Encourage your new husband to contact him and affirm to him that he is not trying to replace him but only wants to be supportive. Let him know you realize that his role as the child's dad is very important and no one will try to take that away from him. Reduce his fears of being replaced.

Try not to criticize him as a father, especially in front of his son. Encourage him when he does something beneficial. Let the child have pictures of dad displayed in his room. Keep the child out of the middle as much as possible. If he has a game, let him invite his dad. You can sit on opposite sides of the field, if necessary. Let him include his dad in his activities—this will lessen dad's fears and keep their relationship alive.

At home, stepdad and son can develop their own relationship. Tell your child you expect him to show respect to his stepdad at all times. If he asks him to do something you expect him to do it. Encourage them to do "guy" things together.

Allow him to keep his relationship with his dad. Children can sense whether their parents are supportive of their relationships or not. Sometimes parents think the other parent is harming their child in some way. Usually it is more harmful for the child to be deprived of parental relationships. Children are resilient but it could take a lifetime to get over being deprived of a relationship with a parent. Don't be the cause of this kind of pain.

Keep the focus off of you and what you want. It is about your child and doing what is best for him. Be respectful of his needs. If your ex spouse continues to name call, etc., then all you can do is set a good example. In the end, your child will make up

122

his own mind about who behaved appropriately and who didn't. He will know you held your tongue and chose to do your best for him. He will respect you and your husband for it. I know this from our experience.

Afterword

A Word of Encouragement

As you invest your trust in God and follow His principles, I know your family will become healthy, unified and enriched. Remember to guard your heart against resentment, unforgiveness, and bitterness. Watch the words you are saying because they will bring life or death. Build relationships with all of your family members and discipline as little as possible until a secure relationship is built with your stepchild.

Love others and treat them like you want to be treated. Treat your spouse's child like you want them to treat yours. If your hope begins to falter, remember the stories of those who have gone before you and now enjoy successful testimonies about their blended family. God is no respecter of persons and what He did for theirs and ours, He will do for yours. And never forget: "All things are possible with God."